OPEN WOUNDS

OPEN WOUNDS

My memoir as a brown-water
U.S. Navy sailor in the Vietnam War

Robert W. Smith
with
Peter F. Morneault

Author: Robert W. Smith
Writer: Peter F. Morneault - www.petermorneault.com

Cover designed by Cathy T. Morneault

Printed in the United States of America
First Printing: 2018

ISBN 9781983260346

For my Sister-in-Law, Catherine Cox, who cared for my family and gave me peace-of-mind during my time in Vietnam.

FOREWORD

Many years have passed since most of us have been in the place called "Nam." Yet, a lot of us still find ourselves trapped in the sights, smells, and sheer terror that was experienced by many in the Brown Water Navy.

A lot of people never knew about us and to this day, many still have no idea of what went on in that hellish place. The Navy was not just ships at sea and aircraft bombing the North. There were many other elements of the Navy that were involved. From the "men with green faces," to the personnel that maintained the choppers, boats, weapons, and provided the many services needed to carry out all our missions. We were not heroes, but just sailors doing our duty the best we could.

Some endured many horrors, some lost several friends in short periods of time. Others were injured in the line of duty and still carry the physical scares as a permanent reminder of that place called "Vietnam." But, no one can take away the fact that the Brown Water Navy was there doing what had to be done in places like My Tho, Can Tho, Ben Tre, Nha Be, Quin Nhon, Cam Rhon Bay, Sa Dec, Tra Cu, and many, many more too numerous to mention.

There were LSTS and many other floating bases that provided the necessary support for many missions in very isolated places. Who can forget TET, or Operation Giant Slingshot? Or, something as simple as searching a sampan and seeing how a family of four or five lived and had their wordly possessions stored in that small boat. How we became familiar with some families to the point that they would always welcome us with a smile, and we would smile back, but always being cautious because this was Nam and things were always happening when you least expected it.

Many days were just boring. Others were filled with sheer terror. Some were just wet and miserable, then there were the days when nothing would go right. I remember pouring water on me and the boat so that I could have a place to sit without burning my rear. Remember how the Vietnamese thought all Americans were doctors? They would bring us their sick and/or wounded. I remember one incident where a young girl had been accidentally hit by a 105 from Dong Tam. Her parents brought her to us all wrapped in a blanket that was soaked with blood. I will never forget what was inside. Only the top part of her body was there from the abdomen up. The sight of that will never leave me.

I am sure that others of the Brown Water Navy have similar experiences and feel the same about a lot of this. For our fellow sailors that gave all, God bless and keep you in His everlasting company. For those of us that survive from day to day with these and more horrible memories, we can hold our heads up high with pride. For we did our duty, and we did it well. No one or anything can ever take that away from us. For all that served in the Brown Water Navy, "Thank You".[1]

Paul W. Cagle
GMG3 - Retired
U.S. Navy

PREFACE

In November 2012, my Son-in-Law, Peter Morneault, suggested that I consider writing a memoir of my experiences in Vietnam. He offered to help me write it, but for years, I neglected to give it a second thought. I never took advantage of his offer.

One morning, while sitting in my favorite chair reading the morning newspaper my eyes locked on to the date. It was July 28, 2017, the 50th anniversary date of my first day in Vietnam to fight in the war.

I out'ta do something about that memoir and let Pete do his thing. I know he'd do a wonderful job.

While talking with my daughter, Cathy, I told her I reconsidered Pete's offer, and I wanted him to write my story. She said, "Pete will be thankful to hear that."

My family needs to read the good, bad, and ugly events I witnessed in Vietnam. My goal is not to glorify the tragic events I saw or experienced. Rather, I want to make my family, friends, and strangers aware of the losses that military families suffered, and the struggles veterans live with daily.

I did and still have a concern about publishing this book because I've included horrific experiences that have haunted me for 50 years.

Skeptics may ask, "How do we know that happened? What proof do you have?" My answer is simple: My integrity. I dedicated 20-plus years of service to the U.S. Navy. I volunteered to die for my country and agreed to protect United States citizens. That's my evidence!

I understand my family and friends may say, "Tell me more about incident XYZ." To them, I will reply, "I have shared as much as I can physically, emotionally, mentally, and spiritually tolerate in this book. I don't want to repeat any incident I have tried to forget for five decades. Thank you for your understanding and respect."

As a reader, you may believe what you want. I did not write this memoir intending to create a historical reference or academic textbook. It's my Vietnam War chronicle. I created a story from letters I wrote to my wife, Joyce over 50 years ago.

With that in mind, I ask you to read this book understanding I used an industry-accepted poetic license to assemble my memories while preserving the authenticity of the overall story.

I would like to thank those who influenced my life during my tour of duty in Vietnam:

The personnel of River Section 532 that I served with between July 1967 and July 1968. Those young men were professional sailors and did their jobs well in trying times.

Lt. Parker, the Executive Officer of River Division 532 was a fine and well-liked officer by every enlisted man in the section. By treating us like men, he kept our morale up in whatever tasks he required us to do. He was fair and exceptional in every way to new sailors and us older guys who had been around for a while.

My courageous young forward gunner, Paul Wayne Cagle, who was a close friend and now lives in South Carolina. He served with me on Patrol Boat River (PBR) 126 and went beyond normal duties to excel in every combat situation. I could always count on him to get a job done, and he earned three Purple Hearts for each serious combat wound he suffered. I also want to thank Paul for the moving tribute he wrote about his fellow PBR sailors and their battles in Vietnam which I included in the Foreword. To this day, I remain very proud to have served with Paul. May God bless him and keep him safe.

I wish to thank my in-laws, Charles and Versie Bailey who insisted that my wife (awaiting the birth of our second child) and son live with them while I served my country. Knowing my family would not live alone comforted me. I am forever grateful for their kindness and support.

My sister-in-law, Catherine Cox, supported my family during my absence. I never concerned myself with their welfare even while my wife, Joyce, gave birth to our daughter. She was there. Cackie, as we call her, also ensured the Red Cross notified me of Cathy's birth. Catherine made sure my entire family was at the airport to greet me when I arrived home from Vietnam. I am indebted to her for the kindness she showed me during the fifteen-months I spent away from home and my family.

My children, Mike and Cathy, for inspiring me to return from Vietnam and be a daddy for them. For making me proud of the adults they became and giving me beautiful grandchildren and grand doggies.

And finally, I thank Joyce for holding our family together during the war. Her strength and positive attitude allowed me to think clearly, with no distractions, and return home safely. She stood by me for 16 years after we married for me to serve our country. Perhaps, our love for one another strengthened during the separations we endured. However, she had one special phrase she would tell me whenever I left for deployment: "If you really love me, you won't go!" As bad as it was, we ended with a kiss goodbye, a smile, and a wave from the pier.

Peter is grateful for the God-given talent he has for writing. He values helping others to feel and express their emotions through his work. Honor fills his soul for the trust Bob and Joyce Smith placed in him by revealing the darkest period of their lives to him. They respected his writing process and allowed him to weave their disjointed memories into a flowing story.

Peter would also like to thank his wife, Cathy, for understanding and supporting his insatiable appetite for writing. He appreciates her enduring patience when he is immersed in the office, with earbuds in, and eyes locked on the screen. Her sacrifices contribute directly and indirectly to his work and this book.

Much of the text in this book is derived from letters I sent to Joyce during my absence. Those letters will appear in an Italic font and as a disclosure, they are not transcribed word-for-word. I omitted sentences, paragraphs, or entire letters pertaining to personal family matters not relevant to this memoir.

I also include explanations to support the letters and that text will appear in a non-Italicized font. Throughout the book, I placed personal photographs and Internet-sourced images used under a Public Domain license.

CONTENTS

FOREWORD I

PREFACE III

INTRODUCTION 1

NOMINATION 5

SURVIVAL, EVASION, RESISTANCE, AND ESCAPE (SERE) TRAINING 9

PBR CLASS 33 15

GRADUATION 27

HARD ENOUGH... 33

MY THREE SWEETIES 49

KIDS IN THE CROSSFIRE 65

AN OPEN WOUND 79

A HORRIBLE HOLIDAY 95

HAPPY NEW YEAR? 103

THE TET OFFENSIVE 117

ANYONE FOR SCRABBLE? 131

JOINING THE ELITE.. 141

NEW SET OF ORDERS 149

SHORT-TIMER'S SYNDROME.. 159

HOME BUT NOT HEALED 167

INDEX 173

INTRODUCTION

The United States faced significant obstacles in its effort to win the Vietnam war. President Lyndon Johnson didn't have military experience, so he trusted General William Westmoreland, who commanded the U.S. Forces in Vietnam.

Johnson's staff and advisers couldn't keep Westmoreland's confidence and arrogance in balance, and they blindly followed his logic, philosophy, and decision-making. Johnson reluctantly sent troops to Vietnam each time the general asked for reinforcements because Westmoreland failed to admit the growing discontent by the general population at home.

His primary strategy was to seek-and-destroy the enemy: find them, engage them on a well-defined battlefield, and overpower them with superior numbers and weapons. In his mind, he could win a war of attrition. However, Westmoreland faced obstacles he didn't expect, and he lacked adequate experience to defeat the spread of communism in Southeast Asia.

He couldn't march U.S. troops into North Vietnam as that action would have prompted China to enter the war, a result the politicians in Washington did not want. The enemy's style of warfare didn't conform nicely into Westmoreland's model of success and they didn't cooperate with his strategy. He was inexperienced in fighting undisciplined soldiers, guerrillas, and communist supporters known as the Viet Cong (VC). Although the Viet Cong soldiers used unconventional tactics, they held distinct advantages over the Allied Forces. Their disorganization and failure to assemble into a formation on a well-defined battlefield proved challenging to Westmoreland.

An impressive fleet of blue-water ships prevented an easy infiltration of the North Vietnamese Army (NVA) into South Vietnam by the South China Sea. A collaboration among the U.S. Navy, the U.S. Coast Guard, and the South Vietnamese Navy formed the Coastal Surveillance Force (Task Force 115) under the code name, *Operation Market Time.*

The NVA and Viet Cong hijacked meek-looking market boats to hide and transport contraband, arms, medicine, and documents into South Vietnam. Task Force 115 used surveillance aircraft to give swift boats, Coast Guard cutters, gunboats, and hovercrafts (shallow-water vessels) specific coordinates to intercept the enemy. In addition, *Operation Market Time* used coastal minesweepers, destroyers, and other deep-water ships to form a blockade against communist infiltration.

North Vietnam, however, used an alternate route to penetrate deep into the heart of South Vietnam. They delivered supplies, via the Ho Chi Minh Trail which traversed through neighboring Cambodia and Laos, countries the United States held a peace agreement with. The NVA utilized a vast network of rivers and canals in the Mekong Delta to deliver supplies to Viet Cong, including the South Vietnam Capitol of Saigon.

Viet Cong guerillas didn't assemble into convenient unified masses. Rather, they mingled in small numbers in the hamlets and among the villagers and farmers, who had no interest in the war. Snipers ambushed, attacked, and quickly retreated into a labyrinth of underground tunnels in the jungle. The VC moved their water taxis, junk boats, and sampans freely on the rivers and canals, places not reached by Task Force 115. They didn't stay long enough to engage their enemy and therefore, were hard to seek-and-destroy. This tactic was effective until the U.S. Navy created a counter-attack strategy.

In December 1965, the Navy developed *Operation Game Warden*, under the command of Task Force 116. Its mission was to patrol, protect, and fight in the muddy rivers and canals of the Mekong Delta. Keeping Saigon's shipping lanes open and free from NVA control was critical. Light and fast crafts could navigate the meandering miles of narrow and shallow inland waterways with ease, but also carry an impressive array of weapons. The problem: The U.S. Navy didn't have such crafts.

Therefore, a civilian manufacturer modified a recreational-use boat to meet the strict needs and standards of military operations. The MK-1 Patrol Boat River (PBR) patrolled the Mekong Delta beginning in March 1966.

Early reports of success for the Navy prompted upgrades to the MK-1. A military contractor mass-produced the MK-2, a top-notch and improved little war boat. However, the boats needed qualified crews.

This is where my journey begins.

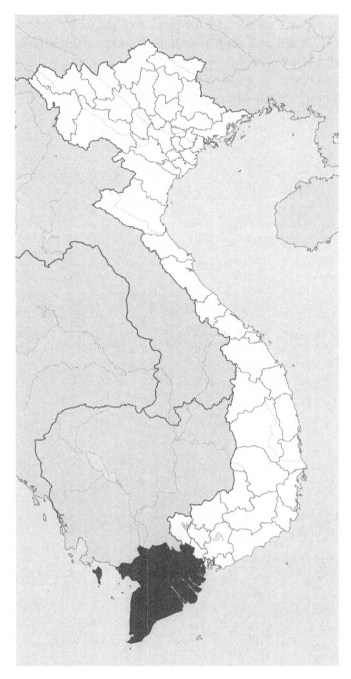

Intro.1: North and South Vietnam. Mekong Delta of South Vietnam highlighted.

NOMINATION

"Joyce, honey—"

"What's wrong?"

"I've got some news that I'm not sure you're going to like. The Navy nominated me for a new assignment."

"Nominated? Well, that sounds exciting."

"Oh, it's exciting alright. The Navy is sending me to Vietnam."

"Vietnam! You're supposed to be on the *Amphion* for two years; it's only been 10-months. We have a baby coming soon. We planned this baby because you would be home."

"I know, sweetie. I ain't happy about it either, but there's nothing I can do about it. Orders are orders."

"When we were in Guam, the Navy sent you to Japan when I was close to my due date with Mike. You missed his birth! You were gone for three months, and I was alone. And now Vietnam! How long will it be this time?"

"12 months."

"A year? What happened to 6-month cruises? How am I going to manage two kids by myself and worry about you getting killed? It's just not fair."

"I'm sorry. We'll find a way. We always do, but that's the Navy for you. We knew this could happen when I reenlisted. We gotta take the good with the bad, and right now it stinks. It'll be rough, especially for you with Mike and another one on-the way. Hopefully, we'll make it through."

"I sure hope so. I don't know how, but you'd better be right."

The Navy selected 150 quartermasters and 150 boatswain's mates for a second wave of patrol boat river sailors to fight in Vietnam. I was a first-class petty officer with a quartermaster (navigator) rating, and I heard about PBRs, but I didn't know much about them. I knew they weren't a typical big Navy ship. The ships in the South China Sea were fairly safe from enemy action, and they had rules-of-engagement to follow.

The patrol boats worked in the rivers without war-tested, pre-established policies and procedures. That was exciting! I wanted to be a part of this new Navy, a brown-water sailor in the rivers–the envy of my blue-water brothers on the shores.

We ain't going on a 6-month cruise across the Atlantic. We're going over to whip some Vietnam ass.

I never considered the opposite could be true.

Image 1.1: Patrol Boat River MK II (PBR) with a four-man crew.

My family accompanied me to Washington Dulles International airport as I prepared to leave for three months of training and eventually a year-long tour in Vietnam. A people mover bus took me out to the terminal. I secured a spot near a window and saw my son, Mike, jumping around just being a 3-year-old. I remember how cute he looked wearing his favorite little red hat. Sadness hadn't overcome me, yet.

I boarded the plane and again made sure to sit at a window. I saw my family, but I wasn't sure they could see me. They didn't leave. Then the emotions flooded over me, and I started sobbing because I was leaving my family. I knew Joyce would be fine because we decided she would live with her parents, Charlie and Versie Bailey. Living in Fairfax, Virginia, she'd live near her only brother, Howard (Butchie) Bailey, and her sisters Catherine Cox, Shirley Price, and Barbara Hurst.

As much as I hoped that I would return in one-piece, I didn't know if I'd ever see them again. I was a real mess.

A flight attendant brought me a shot of whiskey. "Don't cry. This one's on me." I wasn't the only one who received the benefit of her compassion. She prob'ly gave away a whole bottle on that flight.

I arrived at the Naval Amphibious Base Coronado, in San Diego, California on May 10, 1967. I spent a good two days taking care of loose ends like getting a physical, vaccinations, measured for survival training clothes, and other personal needs before my training started.

Sunday, May 14, 1967
Naval Amphibious Base Coronado
San Diego, California

Hi Sweetie & Mike,
Well, it's Sunday, and I have all day to catch up with writing. Now that I've checked in the time is going slow, but I think it will get better when we start school tomorrow. Our first week sounds dull but from what I hear it's not.
I bet Mike wonders where I am now. Has he asked for me? I sure miss you very much, and it hasn't been a week yet. I'm sure we will survive. We always do. There isn't much action, but as the days go by, I will write you when I am lying around the barracks.
Bye for now. I love you both.
Bob

The first week wasn't too boring as they kept us busy with a mix of classroom and physical training (PT). Every morning, we got up early and ran until 7:00 am. Many guys, including me, were out of shape, but I figured after nine weeks we would be in shape, or dead. We'd eat breakfast and start class work in the Vietnamese language and culture.

Writing our last will and testament reminded everyone we were going to war and might not come back. They told us if anything drastic occurred in Vietnam, our commanding officer would send a letter home to our family describing what happened. I didn't like the sound of that, but I guess it was necessary.

PBR Class 33, my class, comprised 50 men in significant-to-PBR ratings: enginemen, boatswain's mates, quartermasters, and machinist mates.

During a break in class, I looked at graduation pictures of all previous classes that hung on the walls of a hallway. While looking at Class 22, I saw my commanding officer (CO) on the *USS Banner*, Captain Lewis. He was a good officer and CO. I respected him because I made first-class petty officer under his command, and Joyce liked his wife. I hoped the PBR training would teach me the leadership skills he had. Like I said, I liked him a lot.

We were the only class in Coronado at the time because Class 32 was training on the patrol boats at Mare Island, in Vallejo, CA. I eagerly awaited getting on those boats, but we had to get through a week of survival training first at Whidbey Island Naval Air Station in Oak Harbor, Washington.

SURVIVAL, EVASION, RESISTANCE, AND ESCAPE (SERE) TRAINING

May 18 - 21, 1967

An instructor handed a fellow trainee a live rabbit after we finished class for the day.

"Alright gentleman, here's your lunch. Or, go down to the river and eat as many clams as you can dig up. Either way, we will give you a knife. Your choice. Enjoy."

Well, I wanted nothing to do with killing a rabbit, so I went clam-digging. I may have found one or two, but I don't remember eating a whole meal. It was our first survival exercise and set the stage for what came later in the week.

I'll never forget one officer in our class who really stood out as a good man. Lieutenant (Lt.) Dennis was a "mustang." He started his career as an enlisted guy and attended Officer Candidate School (OCS) before graduating as an ensign. He understood and related to the enlisted guys in class. It was no wonder he became commanding officer of PBR Class 33.

Our instructors divided us into five columns of 10 men, with the officers grouped separately from the enlisted. They chose a leader for each column, gave him a compass, and instructions. The leader guided his troop through dense woods to three checkpoints within a given time. Our group did well; we passed that test.

The next test proved more difficult to accomplish. We carried white silk parachutes (simulating a downed pilot) to keep us warm while we slept in the woods. Our mission was to evade our enemy who searched for us. We covered ourselves with leaves and branches from the forest floor. However, silk parachutes do not hold debris well and the instructors found us easily. We failed.

May 22-26, 1967

While in formation for roll call, about 10 men emerged from the woods wearing uniforms that resembled a prison guard's. They all shouted at us simultaneously in a foreign language I never heard and couldn't make sense of. They created chaos.

A guard stood two inches from a commander's face and verbally abused him with gibberish. He stepped back and clocked the officer with an open-handed round-house slap which left an imprint of fingers on his cheek. I didn't blame the officer when he tried to retaliate, but the guards violently restrained him. I knew then our training changed tack. No one ever, and I mean ever, hit an officer. If so, he received an ass-woopin', a court-marshal, or both!

A guard got in my face, but I just stared straight ahead. His breath smelled as foul as his attitude. I avoided a slap at first, but he came back, and I took my hit. Every one of us took our licks. They sure put us in a rage; it was enough to make a man spit fire.

That first slap set the tone for the rest of our training that week. I don't believe we were ready either, but we had to take it. The instructors and guards didn't care what pay grade we held or what our rating was. They gave it to the officers more than enlisted guys and acted without fear of retaliation or discipline. Our captors swiftly countered any ill-advised attempts at resistance with an overpowering use of force. I learned to think before I acted on an impulse. I felt like I was playing a game of chess, but war is no game. Plain and simple as that!

Guards assembled us on a gravel road and marched us toward a remote compound. They lined us up in two columns and ordered us to strip to our underwear, tie our boots together, and hang them around our neck. Each man wrapped his arm around the throat of the man in front of him in a choke-hold.

We ran about 100 yards into the compound. We learned quickly that we became prisoners-of-war (POWs).

In the distance I heard the turbo props of an airplane from the naval air station flying toward us. An instructor shouted, "Aircraft!" We jumped into a camouflaged six-foot-deep ditch. The pandemonium of 50 men scrambling into a hole to avoid being spotted by enemy aircraft was dangerous and painful.

Someone landed on me and drove their foot into my ribs and knocked the wind out of me. It was a wonder we survived with only a minor sprain here and there, and of course my aching ribs.

Once we climbed out of the hole, we formed two columns. They forced us onto our hands and knees in a single file. We placed our chins on the butt-crack of the guy in front of us. After being in the woods for days you can imagine we weren't smelling too good. We crawled for about 25 yards, stood up, and gave our rank and serial number. They threw buckets of ice water on us. Although I expected my turn, I was powerless to stop the brutal shock that stopped my heart for a few seconds. I wanted to throw up.

Then they cinched a cloth hood over my head and led me into a building like I was a cow on a leash. They forced me to sit on a wooden chair and removed the hood. I faced a commandant. He was a stupid puke who sat behind a desk and smoked a cigarette. He asked me trick questions, but I only gave him my name, rank, and serial number. Well, that pissed him off, and he ordered a guard to cover my head with the hood. He yanked me out of the chair and walked me about the room for a few feet. They badgered me, getting madder and meaner each time I replied with my name, rank, and serial number.

By this time, they really gave it to me verbally and jerked me around by a drawstring that felt like a noose. I was disoriented and tired, but I never once thought about giving in.

"One more time, Smith. Answer the damn question!"

I didn't give them what they wanted.

The guard screamed into my right ear, "Move!"

He startled the daylights out of me, and I walked straight into a wall that was about six inches in front of me. I hurt my nose, but I didn't bust it open like some of the others.

A guard didn't like my attitude. "You're a tough one, Smith, but we're not done with you yet. You'll give us what we want."

He dropped me to the floor, face down, with my arms extended in front of me. He stood on my hand for about 30 minutes. I guess he tired, because another guard came to relieve him, and he stood on my other hand for another half an hour.

They either ran out of punishment ideas or needed the room to interrogate my classmates because they took me outside and ordered me into a punishment box. The wood box stood about 3-feet high by 3-feet wide with a lid that closed and latched. The confinement wasn't comfortable, but I wasn't claustrophobic either. I kept my wits about me and found a little crack in the box where two of the boards didn't join too well. Positioning myself to where I could at least breathe some fresh air was tricky. I heard the footsteps of an approaching guard as he shuffled across a gravel walkway. My nerves sent chills to my skin as I braced for more torture, but he kept walking. Thankfully.

At night fall, they took me out of the small box and moved me into a 4-foot tall by 3-feet deep box. I didn't have enough room to stand up, but I leaned against a wall and squatted. Some guys were so mentally and physically worn down they had to sit. They received more buckets of ice-cold water and their screams for mercy only wasted more energy. Keep in mind, being in the mountains of Washington state made the water feel extra cold.

Sometimes, the guards dragged a sitter out of the box and beat him with a leather strap. Let me tell you, some of those guards took the punishment too far and really laid into a prisoner. I made out okay I suppose because they only banged on the sides just to make sure I wasn't sitting, sleeping, or dead. No one slept, and we didn't have any water to drink for at least eight hours, and of course no food.

I resisted additional torture by avoiding situations that made matters worse. Any dumb mistake I made in-country could get me killed. I figured the worst day of survival training was easier than the best day of being a real POW.

At daybreak, they assembled us into two unequal-sized groups. I counted 13 men in a small group, leaving 37 in my group. In front of us lied a big pot of stew. Oh, did it smell delicious. We hadn't eaten in a few days, and we hoped to feed our weary bodies. Everyone gathered around the pot with cups in-hand.

"In a few minutes we will let you dip in there and get some chow. You have completed SERE training." At the height of our relief and expectation, the commandant came out of his office and approached our two groups. He kicked over the pot, spilling it all over the ground.

We didn't have enough physical or mental strength to fight or complain. That commandant bastard kicked our spirit and hope for food in the dirt. He left us wondering what misery they would deliver next.

Lies. Expect them, Bob. Never trust anyone!

In that moment, I heard a most glorious sound. The Star-Spangled Banner blared from a speaker behind us. Despite fatigue and frustration, we turned around and saw Old Glory rising. It was a beautiful sight.

The commandant announced with a hint of disgust, "Gentlemen, the nine of you have failed! You are not going to Vietnam." He turned slightly to address the group of 41. "Gentlemen, congratulations. You have successfully passed SERE training and will represent your country well in Vietnam. This concludes your training. Buses will bring you back to the base. Clean up, eat up, and rest up. That is all."

I had no respect for the nine who failed. No one envied them because they would live safely at home and out of the dangers of war. We proudly endured and survived torture and wanted to go to Vietnam. We could trust and rely on our training mates beside us if the shit hit the fan.

Let me tell you, I enjoyed a hot shower and a new set of clothes. We burned our survival clothes, except for our boots. We had to keep them. I will never forget how that stew smelled. I bet it would have tasted just fine too before that jerk kicked the damn pot over. Boy, that made me mad! I sure did stuff myself and slept a good 12 hours. I deserved it because I survived.

The next day they put us on a big bird back to San Diego.

May 30, 1967
Naval Amphibious Base Coronado
San Diego, California

Hi Sweetie & Mike,
I hope you can read this. My hand is still numb. I thought it would be better, but it's not. Bear with me.

After I called you, we went to the airport and flew to San Diego. Well, the plane had engine trouble, so we stayed in Washington another night. We arrived Monday about 1300. We missed a full day of language training, and we will have to study extra hard to catch up. Now we study from 1800 to 2100. They try to cram as much into us as they can.

We listen to Vietnamese tapes through headphones for five hours a day. By the end of school, we should be able to hold a decent conversation.

Honey, as I told you on the phone, that week was rough. I am afraid you will have to wait 'till I can write without pain to get all the details. When I'm able, I promise to tell you about it from beginning to end.

I love and miss you and Mike each passing hour. It was good to hear you on the phone. I wish I could see and hold you both, but we will survive. We always do. As you said in your letter, it is hard at times. With our love for each other, we will be alright in the end.

My mom sent a letter after I got back, and I received four from you. It sure improves my morale to get mail. Tell her about my hand and I will try to write her this week. I know she worries a lot.

About the extra school we'll go to. It shocked us too. It's a 6-week course on Mare Island in Vallejo, CA. We'll learn heavy weapons: recoilless rifles, mortars, and bazooka weapons.

We won't get to Vietnam 'till the middle of September. I'll write more as I learn details.

Honey, I will close now as my hand tires quickly. I love you both and miss you terribly. Bye for now.

All My Love,
Bob & Daddy

PBR CLASS 33

June 1, 1967
San Diego, Cal.

Hi Sweetie & Mike,

I just finished writing to Mom and thought I'd write my "sweeties" again. I just got back from school listening to tapes and my head is buzzing a little yet. Today we learned full sentences at last. Most of this week has been just single words. We are still slow at saying them but we will get better as time goes by. We had a test today and I got a 96 on it. Only 3 failed. They got less than 70.

They are starting to weed out the dead heads now. We started with 50 PBR men and now we have 41 left. Three were dropped

II

Today because they couldn't get this language. They better slow down or we wont have a full crew left to man one Boat. They will cut even more out at Vallo during our boat training. They dont want to send anyone over there so they will end up killing some one. I'm thankful for that.

I'm off all weekend. Me and another 1st Class are going to study most of that time and polish our shoes and just take it easy. We will probly go to the movies on the base at night. They have some pretty good one's here.

Just think honey, one more week and we get out of here. I'll really be glad Too.

III

I'm getting tired of it here. A change of scenery will do us all good. I know the school at Vaiho will be more interesting.

I plan on calling Ken & Judy early next week and try to see them again. Maybe we can have dinner at the Club. But my schedule is so fouled up who knows.

Well Baby & Mike, I will close now and go to bed. You both know I adore you more each day. I miss you more than ever. And love you both terribly much. Tell Mike I love him and to be a good boy. Bye for now.

            All My Love
            Bob & Daddy

June 4, 1967
PBR-33
Naval Amphibious Base
San Diego, CA

Hi Sweetie & Mike,
Just a few lines to say I love and miss you more each day. As today is Sunday, I have plenty of time to write a few letters between studying. Everything is closed, but I will prob'ly see the movie playing tonight.

Tomorrow, we start our last week here at Coronado. Thank goodness. We're tired of going to school and hope it will be more interesting at Vallejo. There are six quartermasters first-class including me, but I only hang around with two of them. We hope to be together in Vietnam, but who knows for sure. Two more guys dropped out during language school leaving 36. There are a few other "dead heads" but I'm sure they won't make it through Boat School.

Has Mike been good, or is he still fighting Robbie? Tell him he had better be nice to Robbie and listen to you, or I won't bring him his big present. Let him know that I love and miss him.

My hand isn't as sore anymore, but I need to get my tape changed tomorrow. I don't think my rib is better, but I hope it heals before we get to Vallejo. Most of us are getting well again, but it's a little slow.

Well love, I will close now. I love you and miss you both. I'll write more again tomorrow night. Bye for now.
All My Love,
Sweetie & Daddy

June 13, 1967
Mare Island, PBR-33
Naval Inshore Op Training
San Francisco Bay Naval Shipyard
Vallejo, CA

Hi Sweetie & Mike,

I got your letter today, and as usual I was glad to hear from you. I enjoyed our talk on Sunday the most though.

Here's a little rundown on the school. It's altogether different from Coronado in San Diego. We sure have all the modern conveniences like a color TV set, a writing desk, bed lamps, and new bunks and big lockers. We're proud of being nominated because they treat us like kings here.

The surface sailors here are envious of PBR crews. The looks on their faces tell us they want to be one of us. We exercise each morning from 0700 'till 0800 for physical training (PT) before we start jogging. While we run, we sing songs as a group and we run everywhere we go. The songs would make you blush as we just make them up and they are raunchy sometimes. On our first day, about 12 guys fell out (quit running), but today we got through it ok. We do this every morning, and I think we will be in good condition when we leave here. Today, we had swimming lessons for most of the day: breast stroke, crawl, backstroke, and some other ones. Every time we got out of the pool we had to do 15 push-ups all together in a group. So, we're tired tonight. Oh yeah, and we had classroom work between rounds of physical training.

We will go on our first operations with the boats on Thursday and Friday 'till about 2200. Saturday, we get more vaccinations, before having the weekend off. Happy days.

Monday starts another week, and we will learn gunnery. They will teach us how to tear down, and put together a M-14 rifle, M-16 rifle, M-79 grenade launcher, and a .50-caliber machine gun. It should be interesting.

I'll buy Mike a nice toy gun when I come home. Tell him he must be a good boy if he wants me to get it for him. I'm sure he is a real mess of a boy. I miss him and you too sweetie, but you both know that.

As it is late and I'm tired, I will close. Bye for now. I love you both more each day.

All My Love,
Daddy

June 14, 1967
Mare Island, PBR-33
Naval Inshore Op Training
San Francisco Bay Naval Shipyard
Vallejo, CA

Hi Sweetie & Mike,
As my days are busy, I consider writing letters to you and Mike as my special time with you. You're all I ever think about.

Today we swam some more, and tomorrow we must qualify as second-class swimmers. We must swim the length of the pool four times and then remain in the water for 15 minutes without touching anything. We tried it today for just five minutes, and it's harder than you can imagine. I hope we can do it, but I guess we'll do our best.

While doing our PT this morning, a bunch of destroyer sailors walked by. Well, we razzed them pretty good. We told them they were in the "candy-ass" Navy, and our instructor heard us call this out. So, he made us do 25 more push-ups than the other classes. There are about 150 PBR men here at the base in three different classes: 31, 32, and 33. PBR 31 leaves for Vietnam soon and 32 is two weeks ahead of us.

Tomorrow we must make our qualifying run. We run three-and-a-quarter miles from our PT field to the swimming pool. We agreed today that it will prob'ly kill us all. I'll let you know how we did. However, the instructors run alongside us. They're the most long-winded bastards I have ever seen in my life. We cuss them under our breaths all the time we're running. But honestly, they are giving us training that could save our lives one day.

Well baby, I will close now. I won't be able to write you again 'till Saturday as we get in late, about 2200 or 2300 at the earliest, tomorrow night. It's our first night with the boats.

I love you both. 'till later.
All My Love,
Daddy

After assembling into formation for our daily run, our instructor surprised us.

"Class 33, I have some good news and bad news for you. The bad news is that we are running further today instead of our normal one mile."

I think the entire base heard our collective groan.

"The good news is you'll get your first look at the boats down at the piers."

Well, that sweetened the bitter pill of extra running. We started hootin'-n-hollerin' and slapped one another on the back.

"Alright, alright knock it off, ladies. Get back in formation and let's get running."

When we reached the piers, I was, what's the right word? Intrigued. Perplexed. I saw a 32-foot long boat without an outboard motor. Instead, two 250-horsepower diesel engines powered Jacuzzi jet pumps to propel it through the water. A fiberglass hull made the boat light and therefore could reach a maximum speed of around 30 knots. Jet pumps allowed the boat to turn 180 degrees in a tight radius, almost within its own length. It also stopped on a dime so to speak and reversed direction within several yards. The boat looked like it should pull water-skiers but carried an impressive array of weapons. I spent time aboard gigantic, grey-painted, slow-and-heavy ships. The boat before me was a fast baby battleship, which was both good and bad.

The fiberglass hulls wouldn't stop a BB gun never mind a VC's weapons. Speed and agility provided its best offensive weapons and heavy guns ensured its powerful defense.

Two .50-caliber machine guns (twin-mounted 50s) lied in the "gun tub" at the front of the boat. A seated forward gunner swiveled in an arc to provide a wide cone of fire. At the rear of the boat, an aft gunner manned a single stand-mounted .50-caliber machine gun. Each PBR had a single stand-mounted M60 machine gun which fired a smaller .30-caliber bullet.

Image 3.1: Speed, agility, and shallow draft of PBR.

Most PBRs in Vietnam carried a modified M79 grenade launcher that mounted on the aft .50-caliber. With a standard M79, a crewman could fire one grenade before having to reload. This was not worthwhile when in a serious firefight. The improved version allowed the crewman, typically an engineman, to fire grenades in rapid succession. Imagine a fictional monkey cranking a handle of an organ grinder. Efficiency and effectiveness of the M79 helped to keep sailors alive. The boats also carried an assortment of grenades: 18-hand, 6-fragmentation, 6-concussion, and 6-white phosphorous. Finally, each crew member armed themselves with an M-16 rifle and the boat captain (coxswain), the 4th crewman, carried a .45-caliber pistol on his hip.

We looked over the boats for about 30 minutes. We weren't allowed on board; that privilege would come in time. Instead, we ran back to the classroom and received additional instruction.

After a few more days of boring school work, they sent us to the infirmary for another round of vaccinations. Our patience wore thin and our bodies ached, so they rewarded us and let us out on the boats.

Most of us did alright handling the boats, but a few caused some minor damage when backing off the piers or coming in too fast. It didn't take much to bang up those fiberglass hulls.

We spent a lot of time on the boats at night because we would patrol the rivers day and night in Vietnam. One night, I drove the boat as we came back toward the piers around 10:00 pm.

Someone asked me a question, and naturally I turned around to answer him. Well, I wasn't paying attention and ran up on a channel buoy about 20 yards in front of us at full speed. I avoided a crash, but I felt a tap on my shoulder.

Oh shit.

I knew our instructor stood behind me. I felt him lean over my shoulder and his bark rose above the engine noise.

"Eyes forward, Smith! You're one lucky son of a bitch. Eyes forward! Your ass would have been history if you hit that buoy. Do yourself a favor. Never lose your focus when you become a boat captain. Otherwise, you're gonna get yourself or someone killed. Got it?"

"Yes, sir." I was thankful that nothing terrible happened, and I sure learned my lesson.

We had a week of mechanical training where we tore apart the engines and put them back together. Talk about a real mess of training. I could tear stuff apart but reassembly didn't come easily because it didn't interest me. Although each crew member had a specific task on the boat, we learned every position in case someone suffered an injury or got killed. I paid attention and learned all about the engines because a fallen boat mate would rely on me someday. He'd want and expect me to bail him out of trouble and vice versa. I never wanted to think, "I wish I paid attention in class. What do I do now?" That could have gotten someone, or me, killed. So, I did my best.

One day during training, each boat driver had to stop the boat, turn off the engines, restart the engines, and then move the boat forward as fast as he could. Well, we watched a boat next to us and saw a guy daydreaming and not holding on to anything. When the boat took off the unsuspecting student fell over the stern and into the water. Our boat picked him up, and we laughed when we dragged him on board. I suppose he learned his lesson too.

June 23, 1967
Mare Island, PBR-33
Naval Inshore Operation Training
San Francisco Bay Naval Shipyard
Vallejo, CA

Hi Sweetie & Mike,
We just finished our last day in engineering (Thank God) so I thought I'd drop you a line or two. As today is Friday, I will prob'ly go to bingo tonight, and hope I win something. We only get to rest on Friday and Saturday because we must polish our boots, belt buckles, and get our greens and equipment cleaned up on Sunday.

By the way honey, we made our 3-mile plus run. Our instructor said we're only the third class to get through without anyone falling-out. We were real proud. We have a reputation as being a good class. All the instructors have told us this. We've knitted into a tight group.

Each morning before our PT, a Marine Corps captain inspects us. Many of the instructors are Marines and they do a good job too as we've learned a lot from them.

PBR class 31 graduated today at 1300. They ran around all morning and razzed the other classes and laid it on thick too. They took our boots outside, tied the laces together in knots, and woke us at 0400. I didn't get the boots on my feet until about 0600. It was all in good fun. We gave them a big send off just before they boarded the buses to go on leave for nine days.

Their class isn't getting heavy weapon training like 33, and the ones that come after us. They're going to a different location in Vietnam than we are. Why, I don't know. We think there is something in the wind, but no one will tell us. I will tell you as soon as I find out something.

I had to laugh when you told me in your letter about what Mike did to Kitty. He is really a pistol. I bet Kitty will stay clear of him from now on. Did you spank him for it? I hope not too hard.

Well Love, I will close now and write to Mom. I love you and Mike with all my heart. I miss you both and you both mean so much to me. Tell Mike I love him and kiss him for me.

Bye for now.
All My Love & Kisses,
Daddy

June 27, 1967
Mare Island, PBR-33
Vallejo, CA

MIKE,

I MISS You AND Love You. I will BRING YOUR BIG PRETTY WHEN I Come Home. TAKE CARE of MOMMIE for ME WHILE I AM AWAY. I HOPE TO SEE you SOON. BE A GOOD BOY AND DONT FIGHT RoBBIE. WRITE SOON

DADDY

Hon,
I thought Mike might get a kick out of getting his own mail. Hope he did.
Love ya
Daddy.

Image 3.2. Jet pumps rather than inboard or outboard motors allowed PBRs to travel at high speed in shallow water. This crew may have wanted to get back in quickly from a long patrol.

GRADUATION

July 2, 1967
Mare Island, PBR-33
Naval Inshore Op Training
San Francisco Bay Naval Shipyard
Vallejo, CA

Hi Sweetie & Mike,
You wouldn't believe how busy we've been. For most of this week, we've trained until midnight or later so we're all pretty beat. It's now 1400, and I just got up. I will go back to bed when I finish this letter because I'm too tired to do anything.

We finished at the range on Friday, and we all got good scores. I was one of seven who made "Expert" as I shot 232 out of a score of 300 on a M-14 rifle.

My commander told me I could get off at 1600 Friday instead of the usual 2200 or 2300. So, I bought my plane ticket today. I will have plenty of time to get my flight, and I will confirm my reservation on Monday. I'm eager to get home.

When we stop in San Francisco, I'll get Mike his present. I know he is just as excited as I am about my coming home. It will be a short weekend, but it's worth it. Then, after all the school is over in August, I will get nine days leave, like Class 31 did. I bet that will go fast too.

Next week, we have more classes on what to expect on the rivers from the Viet Cong. We'll learn how to intercept, board, and search junk boats, water taxis, and sampans. They will also teach us about ambushes, when to shoot, and when not to shoot among other things. You can bet I will not hesitate about shooting when I'm in Vietnam.

Well love, I will close now as I'm still tired and sleepy. I will write more tomorrow. I miss and love you. Tell Mike it won't be long now 'till I am home. Kiss him for me.
All My Love,
Daddy

During the last week of June 1967, we fulfilled our boat driving skill requirement. But, we wouldn't receive our certificates until we qualified in small arms (M-14 and M-16 rifles, 12-gauge shotgun, and .45-caliber pistol). We also had to prove proficiency in big guns (.50-caliber machine gun, M-60 machine gun, and the M-79 grenade launcher).

As a class, we did well, and everyone passed in about two weeks and we earned a U.S. Navy Certificate of Qualification for the PBRs at graduation.

They didn't let us harass and raise hell with the other classes and we didn't get our nine days of leave. The war was serious business, and they needed us immediately in Vietnam. The Navy always made and broke promises and there was nothing we could do about it. I should have expected the change, but not being able to see my family before I left for Vietnam was difficult.

Although PBR Class 33 officially graduated, the Navy sent us to the Philippines for more training. We arrived at Clark Air Force Base, which is about 40 miles northwest of Manilla on July 24, 1967 around 2:30 am. Well, good ole Mother Nature wasted no time exposing us to jungle life because as soon as we landed it rained like crazy. And I mean it was a very heavy rain. We got about three hours sleep and then received a half-day brief before they took us into the jungle for survival training.

A local Filipino guide, assigned to an 8-man group, taught us how to survive and fight in jungle warfare using only a knife. We learned which berries and fruit we could eat and ones to stay away from and how to get water using vines. The hardest part for me was tying together a makeshift bed out of bamboo stalks and vines, so we wouldn't sleep on the jungle floor. None of us mastered that task, but we managed okay.

On our final day in the woods, one of our traps caught a 9-foot boa constrictor, and we ate roasted snake that night. Although it was well-done and tough, it was better than eating berries and fruit.

One guy in a different group got bit on the neck by a two-and-a-half-foot poisonous Bamboo Viper snake. Thankfully, the guide used a walkie-talkie to call a doctor to take him out of the jungle. We all worried for a while, but I never heard anything else about him, so I guessed no news was good news. I don't know if he stayed in the Philippines to recover, or if they sent him back to the States.

We grew tired of training and living from our sea bags like nomads and couldn't wait to fly to Saigon. Settling in one place, starting our jobs, and having normal routines were changes we looked forward to. With all the training I received I felt confident I'd come back to my family in one piece.

We arrived in-country at Saigon's Tan Son Nhut airport at 7:15 pm on July 28,1967. We boarded buses that took us to the Annapolis Hotel, and the sights and smells of a war-torn country quickly overwhelmed me.

Heavy wire surrounded the hotels (military housing) from the ground to the rooftop. The wire kept enemy grenades from blowing up the buildings. Two weeks before we arrived, the Viet Cong frequently launched grenades at the hotels. They wounded six Americans stationed at the Capitol Hotel, just down the street from the Annapolis.

An Army guard stepped from behind a wall of sandbags with a M-16 rifle slung over his shoulder and waved us in. His eyes expressed relief as reinforcement troops came in rather than left. The sense of tension and anxiety smothered me as much as the oppressive heat, humidity, and the mosquitos. Oh, those damn mosquitos were vicious.

We carried a M-16 rifle and two clips of ammunition wherever we went, even to the shower. The VC penetrated Saigon, and we didn't trust anyone, including the people at the Annapolis.

The whole scene confused me, but there I was.

You better adjust, Bob. You're gonna be here a long time.

I followed the directions and advice of the men who had been in-country for a while to a "T" because I figured they survived this long. They were doing something right.

I missed Joyce, Mike, and the baby-on-the-way and I hadn't even been in Vietnam for 24 hours. My 12-month tour was just beginning. I had a long way to go and in a July 28, 1967 letter to Joyce, I wrote, "We realize it has to be this way, or we wouldn't be service people. One day, it will be over, and we'll be together again. So, all we can do is bear with it."

On July 31, 1967, the graduates of PBR Class 33 received the locations of their orders in Vietnam. Boatswain's Mate First-Class Owens and I were assigned to River Section 532 in My Tho (me toe) which is about 50 miles south of Saigon. He was a chain-smoking hick from Arkansas. We weren't exactly friends, but we got along well and that helped us transition to being in-country.

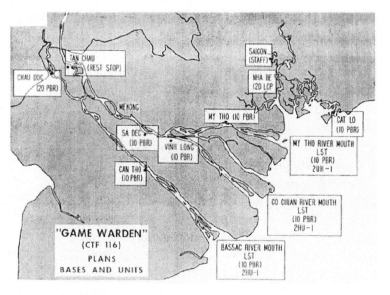

Image 4.1: Operation Game Warden Unit Assignements.

The map above is fairly accurate but not exactly, because My Tho also supported 10 PBR boats from River Section 534. I never kept track of my classmates who spread out among the nine or ten river sections throughout South Vietnam. I focused on keeping my own butt alive and the men in 532 and 534.

Owens and I had problems getting to My Tho at first because our arrangements kept falling through. Thankfully, we found a helicopter pilot who was heading south, and he let us hitch a ride.

We couldn't land in My Tho because the VC was attacking the city. So, they dropped us down in a little city called, Ben Tre.

From there we rode a water taxi across the Mekong river with people, pigs, cows and anything else that fit on there. Section 532 personnel greeted us and escorted us to meet our commanding officer (CO).

Around 6:00 pm, the CO sent us to chow, and we checked in later to the Carter Hotel across the street from the headquarters. The hotel carried the name of a killed-in-action (1966) 532 PBR sailor.

We slept four to a room, and although we had a sink and a shower, we didn't have hot water. So, I adapted to cleaning up with just cold water.

Adjusting to our daily commute wasn't easy either. Like the hotels, heavy-gauge wire covered the jitneys (small and rickety buses) that brought us to and from the piers and our barracks. We worried about the VC killing us with grenades before and after spending 12 hours on patrol. It was unnerving to say the least. I've never been in a prison cell before, but it sure felt like I was living in one every day. Welcome to Vietnam!

Image 4.2: Mekong Delta.

HARD ENOUGH

August 6, 1967
My Tho
Mekong Delta, South Vietnam

Hi Sweetie & Mike,
It's been almost a week now since I've had a chance to slow down. I will try to fill you in.
We've spent most of the week on patrol. We've been on three day-patrols, and three night-patrols so far, with each one about 12-14 hours long. Well, in six patrols we've been shot at twice, both by a sniper. We put enough .50-caliber slugs in his general direction that he didn't fire any more. We don't know if we killed him or not. We also caught three Viet Cong trying to cross the river. The one VC we caught last night didn't have an I.D. card and no manifest papers. He tried to take 30 bottles of morphine and penicillin to his fellow VC across the river. We confiscated the bottles and took him to an outpost on the river. Many of the outposts are manned by Vietnamese, who have lost family members to the Vietcong. You can prob'ly guess what will happen to him.
The town of My Tho is of medium population. It has about 20,000 people - about 8,000 are VC that mingle into the civilians living here. As you can see, we don't know who is who. The Vietnamese 7th and 9th Army of the Republic of Vietnam (ARVN) are stationed here and keep My Tho fairly secure.
All the PBR sailors wear black berets. I will get pictures as soon as I can and send you some. Boy, do we look sexy in greens and black berets.
Our mail isn't the best sweetie, but it finally gets here. They have had two mail calls in a week and I sure hope it improves.
I will write as much as I can between patrols. I miss and adore you both. This will be a long year, but we will love each other more when it's over. Tell Mike to be good and kiss him for me.

I will close now as we must go to a briefing on our patrol area,
I'll write again later. I miss and love you with all my heart.
Bye for now.
All My Love,
Me

I rode along as a fifth member of various boat crews because I was training to become a boat captain. After all, the Navy chose me for that position a few months earlier. When we patrolled, we always went in a pair of PBRs. We stayed tight to each other to provide firepower (cover) if the second boat came under attack. But, we wouldn't stay so close that the VC could kill-two-birds-with-one-stone.

To avoid an ambush along the riverbanks, we searched boats in the middle of the river, away from potential enemy fire coming from the jungle. One boat would search and check IDs while the cover boat had their guns ready in case the boat was hiding a VC who had any funny ideas.

Image 5.1: I took this picture while our boat provided cover. A Vietnamese policeman/interpreter boarded the sampan and checked IDs and papers. No real concerns here. Routine stop with cooperative market-goers.

We would fire a warning shot in front of a boat we wanted to search. We'd gesture for the boat to approach us in the middle of the river. For the most part, the villagers understood what we meant, and they would come to us and let us search without any problems.

Sometimes, that plan didn't work out too well.

August 8, 1967
My Tho, Vietnam

Hi Sweetie & Mike,
Now that I have a few minutes before we go on patrol I thought I would drop you and Mike a letter. I hope you got my other one.

Yesterday on patrol, a bad and sad incident happened on my cover boat. The boat captain on my cover boat killed a six-year-old boy riding in a water taxi.

Here's how it happened. The boat captain fired his warning shot into the water, but the bullet took a bad bounce and hit the boy under the left armpit and came out the other side. He died right away. We felt sorry this happened but there was nothing we could do. The Navy will take care of the family somehow.

Just before our relief boats came yesterday we were called for a medical evacuation (medevac). The VC set off a mine in a village, and we picked up the injured. There were two dead and seven wounded when we arrived. We loaded up the seven people (five kids) and started back to My Tho with them. A girl, about nine years old, had her foot blown off. I held a boy of about six years and he gurgled a little when I tried to give him water. He died right in my arms. I laid him back down, covered him with my raincoat, and immediately threw up over the side of the boat. For about an hour afterwards, I didn't feel too well. I must learn to control my emotions better than I think I have. This is a nasty war, and it's a shame the kids are suffering.

How's all at home? Fine, I hope. I miss you and Mike. Tell Mike I'm sending him a beret just like Daddy wears soon.

My face is peeling because of the sunburn. Boy, do I look terrible. The guys call me a leper. I hope it will clear up. I don't have to worry about my arms; they are already brown.

Our mail came yesterday. I didn't get any but maybe I will soon. The VC keep blowing up the roads and bridges the mailman uses. I guess old "Charly" (VC) took a break yesterday and let the mail get through.

We have a small group of U.S. Army Advisers to the 7th Viet Army stationed about five miles from here. Their base sells cigarettes and soap and stuff that we can buy. We get our haircuts across the street in a small barbershop. When we're not on patrol, most of us sleep because we lack it the most.

Tell Mom I'll write her soon as I can. I miss and love you and Mike something awful. Kiss him for me. I will close now but will write more soon. Take care of yourself and the baby.

Bye for now.

All My Love,

Me

In September 1967 we increased our presence on the rivers because of the Vietnamese elections. We received intelligence reports indicating the VC would ramp up their terror attacks. We caught at least one, sometimes two, VC boats during our day patrols.

If we found a boat trying to cross the river after the curfew of 8:00 pm, we just shot them because we knew they were VC, and we didn't take any chances The legitimate fishermen and market boats learned to stay off the rivers at night.

During our months of training before arriving in Vietnam, our instructors drilled it into our heads, "Don't fire at the enemy unless first fired on." Well, once we were in-country and out on the rivers, we didn't follow those directions. It was all a bunch of bologna! We never did that.

When I saw the ruthless VC kill small children, it really shook me up. Having a little boy die right in my arms left one hell of an open wound. I will never forget that moment. Never.

War is nasty and ugly, but the higher-ups said we had to receive fire before we could retaliate. I don't think so. We'd shoot first and say the hell with it. We didn't pay attention to the Rules of Engagement bullshit. And it was all bullshit too. Do you think the VC followed those rules when they killed children and tried to blow us up? Hell no. I'm sure neither the Army, nor the Marine Corps paid attention to it. There are no rules in war. We couldn't wait 'till we got killed before we fired back. What good is that? It was just plain stupid, and our officers knew it too.

You see, we went out on patrol every day, but most of the officers didn't. I'm not taking anything away from them, but they could have gone on more patrols than they did. We seldom saw an officer out on patrol because they only needed to complete two patrols each year. Two patrols in a year! It was absolutely ridiculous. We put our butts on the line every day and most of them sat around doing a bunch of nothing. They stayed on base and pushed papers all day. When an officer did patrol, he avoided trouble and kept to the middle of the river. Except Lt. Dennis, our CO of PBR Class 33 back in the States. He patrolled the rivers nearly every day. He was a gung-ho guy who earned and didn't demand our respect. But, to the other officer's credit, they never put pressure on us. They let us do our thing, within reason.

August 13, 1967
My Tho, Vietnam

Hi Sweetie & Mike,
Now that it's Sunday and I have the day off, I'll write a few lines to give you what little news I have.

I just finished another night patrol, and we got a little excitement as we came in. We figured we survived another patrol, and we were shooting the breeze. Good ole Charly fired a single mortar round at us when we were almost in. It hit in the water about 100 yards astern of the boat and the shrapnel put a hole or two in the boat. Thankfully, no one got hit, but it sure scared the hell out of us. We can't drop our guard over here for a minute.

Remember I told you of the small group of Army Advisers about five miles from here. Well, the VC shelled them with mortars and fired automatic weapons at them for about an hour last night. We watched the tracer bullets fly and the shells hit from out on the river. The outpost was too far inland for us to help them, but we had a ringside seat and heard all the action on our radio. It looked like the 4th of July with all the shells going off. Thankfully, no one was hurt.

I don't go out again until tomorrow at 0530. I enjoy the day patrols better than the night patrols because we stay busy searching junks and sampans and time passes faster. You would have laughed at me the other day. I boarded a water taxi and a young woman about 20-years old gave me her ID card. She checked out okay. Then, I looked in her bag and she only had two braziers in it. I took one out and held it up to my chest. Everyone laughed like hell. She really turned red. I even had to laugh at myself. About half the people on the river are VC, and I know some were on the taxi. It just goes to show you the VC can laugh too.

Image 5.2: Water taxi. The local villagers loved when we gave them our sea rations. They'd sell them at the market. On occasion, they'd volunteer information about the VC in exchange. We built a good relationship with them.

The whole town is decorated with Viet flags and posters for the election. We are expecting trouble but hope there won't be any. We won't leave the hotel area for a few days during the election just to be cautious.

I hope you're feeling good and don't have any trouble with the baby. 'Till I hear from you, I will be concerned. I sure miss you and Mike more each day and I know you feel the same. One day all this will be over.

Sweetie, I will close now and go to dinner at the mess hall. I love you and Mike with more than words can say in a letter. I will write more later.

Bye for now.
All My Love,
Me

August 15, 1967
My Tho, Vietnam

Hi Sweetie & Mike,
Just a few lines to tell you how much I love and miss you both as I go on patrol again at 1730.

Last night, a sampan shot up a Section 532 boat while trying to cross the river, but they didn't hit anyone. They turned around and retreated to the riverbank. PBR boat # 126 (PBR 126) killed three VC in the sampan. They didn't stop to take the dead ones with them. The crew seized some papers and two automatic weapons in the sampan. I went down to the pier this morning to look at the damage and saw six bullet holes in the bow, and one in the windshield. The crew also captured a VC flag that we will hang in the club. So, when we get drunk we can cuss and throw beer bottles at it. Haha.

I don't remember if I mentioned the club to you or not. It's a two-room affair that they are remodeling. They will reopen on Saturday the 19th of August. I look forward to coming in from patrol and having a cold beer. Beer is 10 cents a bottle, or should I say can. We will also have a TV, pool table, and a big shuffleboard.

Word is going around they may move our section headquarters further downriver to a big Landing Ship Tank (LST) that is anchored at the mouth of the Bassac River. We like it here, but we will just have to wait and see.

I know for sure time is going by quickly. Maybe it's because we patrol a lot. I hope the rest of it goes by this fast too.

Honey, I figure I will prob'ly save about $1000 or even $1500 while I'm here if they ever get my pay squared away. They pay us on the 24th of each month. I will see what I draw this payday to figure how much I'll put in savings. Whatever it is, it will surely come in handy.

Tell Mike I will send his beret this payday if all goes well. Kiss him and tell him I miss and love him. I will close now, Sweetie. I adore you and hope all is ok with you and the baby. More later.

Bye for now.
Your Sweetie

August 16, 1967
My Tho, Vietnam

Hi Sweetie & Mike,
Not much new here except it's hot as hell, and it rains day and night. The rainy season should be over now, but it may have another month to go.

Don't worry about me not getting your mail, Sweetie. I talked with an officer today, and he told me nobody gets their mail right away when they first get over here. He said he waited three weeks and then he got it all at once. So maybe I'll get some soon, huh?

I am now boat captain of PBR 126. The other boat captain went on emergency leave. We don't think he is coming back as he had about 45 days left here.

A hillbilly band is playing down at the piers tonight from 2000 'till midnight. I won't go because I must go on patrol. Besides, I don't care for hillbilly music anyway.

I will make this a short letter as there isn't much to say. Remember Honey, I love both of you very, very much and can't tell you how much I miss you.

Bye for now.
All My Love,
Your Sweetie

After a month of boat captain training, I finally got my own boat and crew. I stayed in the same room as my crew, and we spent the first couple of days getting to know one another. I had a Texan, a Native American Indian from a Ute tribe out west somewhere, and an Irishman in my room. Some combination, huh?

There's nothing like a firefight to test the potential of a good relationship with your crew. During our first firefight, everyone performed flawlessly. Their ability to breakdown and clean the .50-cals impressed me. The forward gunner needed brute strength to operate the turret-mounted twin 50s. Each gun weighed at least 100 pounds and swiveling the gun tub required manual power.

Image 5.3: I'm hamming it up atop the forward gun tub with the twin 50s and a grenade. Radar dome is above the canopy over the coxswain's flat.

Thankfully, stop-blocks halted the panning and firing momentum of the turret. Otherwise, those machines gun would literally cut a crewmate in half with bullets. The later model, MK II PBRs added a hydraulic system which made the forward gunner's job much easier.

My forward gunner, Paul Cagle, a third-class gunner's mate, was a good man. Although quite young, maybe 19 or 20-years old, he felt compassion for the Vietnamese and always stepped up first to help the wounded civilians. I liked his sense of humor too as he tried to keep things light on patrol. He was a crew member I always trusted and counted on.

Nester was my tolerable engineman and M79/M60 guy. At times, he could be a loose cannon and a real pain in the ass. I don't remember the names of my other two crew members, but at least I don't remember them as being incompetent or real jerks or anything like that.

A 32-foot boat didn't offer too many places to hide, so we learned to get along. On a small boat with four other men, no one tolerated an I-want or Me-first attitude. I can't speak for others, but I was a career Navy man. Serving just my obligatory four years and bailing out didn't work for me. I already tried that. The Navy life kept me happy as strange as it may sound. The younger guys sometimes showed their maturity and partied downtown or chased women around after getting in from patrols. Without a wife and kids at home, they thrived on excitement and stupid ideas. Getting off the boats and walking into the jungle to seek-and-destroy some "gooks" was a favorite pastime for them. I didn't support or tolerate that behavior. Their lack of common sense and constant desire to defy orders didn't sit well with me because their immaturity could have gotten me killed.

Thankfully, I had a good crew, and we got along well enough, although we were in a war, we occasionally enjoyed a good laugh.

I remember being on a day patrol, and the VC must have been resting or something because the river was quiet. Well, Nester kept himself busy and cleaned the M79 grenade launcher between his legs with the barrel pointing straight up toward the sky.

A very distinct sound rose above the sound of the humming diesel engines.

THOOOMP.

Cagle, with panic in his voice asked, "Nester, was that thing loaded? Son of a bitch! Smith get us the hell out of here. Nester just launched a damn grenade!"

I too heard the unmistakable sound of the M79, but I didn't waste time asking questions. I jammed both throttles forward into the dashboard, knocking my other three crew members off balance. Each one let out a startling, "Uggh" or "Aaah" before they hit the deck with a heavy thud.

I shouted over the noise of the two now-roaring diesel engines, "No time for apologies boys!"

Nester unintentionally left a grenade in the M79 and somehow hit the trigger. What goes up must come down. The grenade landed and sent a tremendous plume of shrapnel and water high into the air, showering the area where we had just been.

Once our adrenaline calmed down we had a good laugh.

I told Nester, "You dumb shit! It's hard enough to stay alive out here without blowing ourselves up."

It was a mistake any of us could have made. Boy, did we ever get lucky. Nester felt horrible and we didn't help matters by razzing him for the rest of our shift. Nester was never quite the same after that incident. He didn't lose his mind, but I think it shook him up real bad. Perhaps, it hurt him like an open wound because events happened that we just didn't forget. We never wanted to make the same mistake twice, so we lived every day with anxiety. Like I said, we got real lucky.

All in all, I had a good bunch of guys on my boat, and I hope they felt the same about me. Nester would later get his revenge on me.

August 20, 1967
My Tho, Vietnam

Hi Sweetie & Mike,
Well, my morale just jumped up 100% because I got a letter and the sports section from you and a letter from Mom. You

mailed it on the 12th, and I got it the 19th. I'm glad I got some mail. Honey, I can't tell you enough how relieved I am that you, and the baby are ok. I worry about that you know, and I will 'till I'm a daddy again, and all is ok.

I'm sending you a picture (which I don't think is very good) that was taken out on the river. We were coming in and waiting for another patrol to relieve us.

Image 5.4: Coming in off patrol wearing a beret and a rare smile. Battered American flag waving in the top left corner of picture. Roost of water behind me indicates we were moving fast. Second boat in our patrol was in front of us. We may have even been racing.

I plan to get a couple of rolls of film and borrow a camera from one of the guys in my boat crew and take some good pictures.

Our living conditions surprise me. We have movies every night, plus TV of all the good shows from the States. Some of them are: Bonanza, Dick van Dyke, Big Valley, Lorado, Green Acres, plus all the sports. We see a baseball game every Saturday, and I just watched a football game between the Los Angeles Rams and New Orleans Saints. They are at least a week or so old, but they do what they can to make it pleasant for us.

The VC we caught with the morphine and penicillin (August 6 letter) got the medicine from North Vietnam. The Viet Cong bastards literally took a boat-load of medicine to Hanoi, in a boat from the United States. I don't know how he got it, but the Navy traced it down and told us.

Oh, about the VC we caught. The South Vietnamese police killed him in their station after they got valuable information from him. The policemen kill all the VC we catch unless he is a big wheel or something.

We got some bad news today. The VC wounded one of our men and killed an ensign during an ambush in the northern patrol area. The boat was relieving another one when a sniper fired at the boat. The ensign took a bullet through the back and the guy driving the boat (a boatswain's mate first class) was shot through the jaw. It took half his tongue off. They flew him out right away, but we don't believe he will ever talk again.

Last night on my patrol, we found a sampan with an 8-month-old (I'm guessing) dead baby on board. It must have been on the river for two or three days because the body was really dark and stiff. We took it to an outpost for burial.

Well Sweetie, I will close now and hit the sack. I miss you and love you more than words can say. Tell Mike to be good and mind Mommy. Kiss him for me. I'll write more later.

Bye for now.
All My Love,
Your Sweetie

August 27, 1967
My Tho, Vietnam

Hi Sweetie & Mike,
Boy, did I hit it good again today. I got three letters from you. It sure makes me feel good to hear from my Sweetie.

Two nights ago, a Navy photographer came down to our base, so he could ride with us. He hoped to get some pictures of a medical evacuation (medevac) for the Stars and Strips newspaper. If someone gets shot, steps on a mine, or wounded we medevac them to My Tho. Well, he got a lot more than he imagined he would.

Our two-boat patrol went upriver about 15 miles north of My Tho. We cut our engines and drifted downriver with the current.

We figured if the VC couldn't hear our engines, we'd catch them in an ambush. Well, we did this but didn't see anything the first time. So, we went up again and picked up two dots on our radar while drifting downstream. They didn't see us, but we saw two sampans loaded with VC appear about halfway across the river.

It was so funny now that I think about it. We drifted right up on them. We got ready to open fire on them, and then we turned our searchlights on them. If you could have seen the looks on their faces, they would have made you laugh too. Their expressions seemed to say what General Custer said at the Little Big Horn. "God damn, look at all those Indians." Only they said look at all those PBRs.

We closed within 10 yards from their boats when we opened fire on them. My cover boat took one sampan, and my crew took the other. We killed nine VC in the boat we fired at, and the other boat killed five, and captured three more. We also got two machine guns, and a pistol out of what remained of the sampan. After we quit firing and got the sampan alongside, we searched it for more arms and important papers. Well, this prob'ly sounds gruesome to you, but we have to do this. As we got in the sampan to search the bodies, one VC was leaning over the side of the sampan with three bullets in his side. One of my guys said, "Look at that son of a bitch. He's dead but won't close his eyes." So, he shot him again to make sure. Blood covered us from head to toe after we searched the bodies. Even our shoes soaked in puddles along the bottom of the sampan. After we searched them, we threw them in the river. We aren't allowed to bring them back to My Tho.

After we got in from patrol about 0630 the next morning we went to the club. Most everyone was having coffee and donuts, but they broke out six cases of ice-cold beer for the two boat crews. We talked all morning and got drunk as skunks. Everyone wanted us to keep telling the story of what happened, so we did. You know how people are.

Oh, by the way, the photographer got so excited with all the action that he dropped his camera in the river and burned his arm on a HOT barrel of a .50-caliber machine gun. We had to laugh at him. He wrote a good story though for the paper. It should be out soon.

How are you feeling now? Fine, I hope. I hope you realize I don't want to write about all that mess, but you said you didn't want me to keep you in the dark.

As today is Sunday, I will prob'ly go watch the ball game at the club. The White Sox are playing the Twins. I also see the Redskins beat the Bears on Saturday afternoon.

Well baby I will close now and go to lunch. I adore you both and miss you too. Kiss Mike for me. Take care and I will do the same.

All My Love,
Your "Sweetie"

August 29, 1967
My Tho, Vietnam

Hi Sweetie & Mike,
Another letter arrived from you again today, so while I have the time I will answer it.

I'm glad you talk to Mike and tell him about his daddy. I surely miss him a lot and you too. Tell him I bought his beret today and will send it to him tomorrow ok? And tell him to be good, mind you, and I love him.

On my last patrol, a Viet riverboat killed a woman in a canal. I wrote a statement on it and I am sending a copy to you. I had to write this statement because if I didn't the Viets would try to blame the PBRs for killing her. Her son, who was in the boat with her, didn't blink an eye or cry when she died. These people don't have any feeling at all like us Americans.

She had a big hole in her neck too. She was a real mess. A bullet from a machine gun sure makes a mess of a person.

I go back out again tonight and stay 'till 0600 tomorrow morning. We will patrol a new river that we haven't patrolled for two or three months. Maybe we will run across some VC huh?

I will send some pictures soon as I bought film yesterday and one of my crew is letting me use his camera. I hope they turn out well.

Well love and Mike, I will close now and get a little sleep for tonight will be a long one. I love you and Mike dearly and miss you. I will write more later.
Bye for now.
All My Love,
Your Sweetie

28 August 1967

UNSWORN STATEMENT OF ROBERT W. SMITH

As Boat Captain of PBR 126, based at My Tho, Vietnam, during a routine morning patrol at 1000 hours on 27 August 1967, I observed the following which resulted in the death of one (1) Vietnamese female civilian. While searching a water taxi at the west end of the Cua Dia a sampan was observed crossing from west to east, about 500 yards from PBR 126. Upon observing this sampan, three (3) warning shots were fired in the air to alert the sampan to come along side PBR 126. Either the sampan did not hear the warning shots, or did not heed them. The sampan proceeded across the river and entered a small canal at coordinates 609 385. On firing these warning shots, two Viet FOMS were observed passing PBR 126 and the water taxi. The Viet FOMS increased speed and headed in the direction of the crossing sampan. The Viet FOMS it was observed passed close in to the canal the sampan entered. The PBR cover heard approx. 100 rounds of M. G. fire from the FOMS which did not stop, and continued to pass the entrance to the canal. PBR 126 has finished searching the water taxi and proceeded to the entrance of the canal. Upon arrival there, the sampan was observed coming out of the canal. A small boy, about 9 years old was waving his arms to get our attention and hollering something in Vietnamese. The sampan came alongside PBR 126 and it was observed that a female Vietnamese was sitting up in the forward part of the sampan bleeding perfncely from an obvious gunshot wound. I immediately jumped into the sampan and observed she had been shot through the right side of the neck just below the cheek bone and the bullet coming out the left cheek. She was still alive, but had lost consideral amount of blood and was continuing to bleed very badly. SN LOTT our forward gunner and I lifted the woman out of the sampan into PBR 126, to give first aid and try to stop the bleeding. As she was lying on PBR 126's engine cover she died. We covered her over with a poncho and requested instructions from My Tho. We were instructed not to deliver the body to My Tho. Meanwhile, the Viet FOMS had come within 10 yards of PBR 126 and were looking into the boat at the body. The Viet FOMS then turned around and continued down river. We delivered the womans body and her son to Giao Hoa outpost coordinates 508 377 and left them there. At 1100 we were back on station.

ROBERT W. SMITH

WITNESS:

She died 3 minuty after I got her aboard.

P. S.
the women was not a VC. love "me"

Image 5.5: A formal report I submitted declaring I was not responsible for a Vietnamese (not VC) woman's death.

MY THREE SWEETIES

September 2, 1967
My Tho, Vietnam

Hi Sweetie & Mike,
Since I've not written in a few days and I have time, I will send you a note. They doubled the number of patrols we must go on 'till after the elections. They expect the VC to be active today and tomorrow. Yesterday, our patrols reported there was hardly anyone on the rivers. The VC told the local people they better not vote, but they did last year, and I think they will again this year. We're glad it has been quiet, and I hope it stays that way.

Yesterday, I took 20 color pictures while out on patrol. As soon as I get them back, and if they turn out, I will send them to you. Most of them are of me. Haha. Tell Mike there are lots of guns in them too. I also bought his hat and a river section patch for him yesterday after I came off patrol. I will send them to him real soon.

The ensign who was killed, visited from Saigon and asked to go on a patrol. So, they let him, and it wound up being his last one. He wore his flak jacket, but Honey, they only slow down a bullet. They are designed to protect against shrapnel, not stop bullets. However, people have told me many times they can save your life.

The boatswain's mate wasn't in my PBR class. He was in Class #30 and had been here about two months.

I'm glad you're doing fine with the baby. Take care, and don't lift anything heavy, but I don't need to worry about you not taking care of yourself. I'll be glad to get word that I'm a daddy again and all is fine, and it's a girl. I know we both want a girl this time. So, let's keep our fingers crossed ok?

This is my boat crew until they leave. All of them are short timers and will leave in less than 30 days. After that I will get a new crew.

Mail call will have already gone when I get in from patrol, but I should get some from you. I sure like hearing about things at home. Will you send the sports section occasionally? I would enjoy reading about the Senators and Redskins.

Well, I will close now and go get a shower (cold of course.) I'll write again tomorrow. Remember you're both thought about every minute and I love you both.

Bye for now.

All My Love,

Me

3 Sept 1967

Hi Daddy,

She is here and just beautiful. I only wish you could be with me. Our "baby sister" looks just like her big brother. Honestly Honey, she is the picture of Mike.

I surely didn't waste any time having her. She came faster than Mike. My labor didn't start until 1:00 a.m. Today so I wake up Mom and told her I had a backache and it was regular at about 5 minutes apart. I thought it might be false labor but Mom called Cackie and she came up and called the doctor, then my pains were a little harder and it was very difficult for me to sit when I had one so Cackie said I had better go in the ambulance. She called the firehouse and Jim Stewart and Butchie came down

?

to get me. Butchie was scared to death! Jim rode in the back with me and Butchie drove "FLEW". He wasted no time at all, with red lights and the siren. I guess he thought I might have her before we got to the hospital. Had I waited any longer, I just might have too.

Oh my how, I was checked in and the doctor saw me at 2:30 am and he said "I'll have someone for you by 3:00 o'clock". Well, our Cathy came at 3:04. It was an easy delivery and I feel better than when I had Mike and I felt very good then. I am so very lucky to deliver so quickly and easily. My roommate was in labor 18 hours.

Poor Dad didn't even know I had left for the hospital until Cackie called them to say our girl

3

had arrived. He said "Why in the Hell didn't you wake me up". We didn't really have time to.

I called Mike this morning and Honey, he was so excited. He said "Is my baby sister out of your stomach? He just kept pouring out the questions. He wanted me to come home today and bring her. I asked him if he remembered what we named her and he said quickly "Cathy" - "Do you like her". I had to laugh at him I think he would have talked all morning if I could have stayed on the phone. I'm anxious to see his face when Cathy and I go home.

I hope you got the telegram from "Mike" okay I was so anxious for you to know about your daughter's birth. Just think Honey, you did it all and I love you so much for our new baby and such a darling little girl at that. How is only I can keep everyone from spoiling her, maybe she will be as good a baby as Mike was. I'm sure going to try.

Your Mom is supposed to come see me this afternoon. I don't know who else. I think my folks are coming tonight with Cookie.

I hope you didn't eat any beer coasters upon learning the news like you did with Mike's birth. I bet you had a few cold ones though - but I hope you did anyway.

Well, Daddy, I will stop now as I'm a little tired. Hope you can read this as I'm not in the best of writing positions.

Take care Sweetie, I'll write more tomorrow. Be careful and we all three love you extra specially.

Our Love + Kisses to Daddy
Mommie, Mike + Cathy

September 4, 1967
My Tho, Vietnam

Hi Sweetie & Mike,
As I must go on patrol tonight, I'll write a few lines while I can. I got another letter from you today and it sure makes me feel good to get mail.

Yesterday one of our boats had a good day. They killed six VC and confiscated two Chinese, two Russian, and two American M-16 rifles. So, you can see they have a variety of weapons.

The weather here is hotter, but at night we sleep with a sheet to keep warm. It's cooler here than in Guam for sleeping.

The river was quiet during the voting yesterday. We had no trouble from the VC. I don't know who won or how many people voted.

The day before yesterday, we got word over our radio to support an outpost that was under attack. So, we went downriver about eight miles to help them, and you would have thought it was the fourth of July with all the fireworks.

The Air Force sent six jets in, and they tore up the beach when we got there. They had already dropped Napalm, and the banks burned like crazy. We stayed out in the middle of the river when they fired their rockets. Two of them fell short and landed about 100 yards from us. It scared the devil out of all of us.

A helo came down and told us to move out of the area, so we did. We didn't want to end up as a friendly-fire casualty. Besides, we only had 200 rounds of .50-caliber ammunition left. Those gun barrels were hot. The VC didn't return fire from the beach, but we don't know if we killed any of them. We sure made it hot for Charly if he was in the area. I'm sure higher-ups will give us a report soon. They didn't overrun the outpost though, so we did our job well I guess.

Well baby, I will close now and catch an hour or two of sleep before I go on patrol. I love you and Mike more each passing day. And each one that passes means I will get home that much faster.

Bye for now.
All My Love,
Your Sweetie.

September 9, 1967
My Tho, Vietnam

Hi Sweetie, Mike & Cathy,
Today, you've made me the happiest person alive. When I read your letter about Cathy coming I felt so good I couldn't talk. I told everyone I saw about the wonderful news. I even told the Vietnamese workers in the hotel, but they stared at me like I was a nut. They didn't understand a word I was saying, but I didn't care.

I bought two boxes of cigars at the Army base and have shaken 60 hands or more today. Everyone here is happy for us. She's just beautiful, isn't she? I wish I could see her and hold her in my arms. Send pictures as soon as you can. Mike is prob'ly a real mess and just as excited as me, and I won't meet her for almost a year which will be hard!

Did Butchie drive 90-miles an hour getting you to the hospital? Was he scared? How long did it take you to get to the hospital? I bet Charlie was a nervous wreck too. I can hear him now, cussing like he does.

This is the first word I got about the baby being born. If Saigon received a telegram, they didn't forward it to me. They mess up a lot there. It's a wonder how they keep track of the condition or location of anyone when they always lose people, records, etc.

Anyway Sweetie, I realize it's not anyone's fault at home, and the only thing that matters is knowing all is well with you and Cathy.

Honey, since reading this letter I can hardly write. I want you to know I adore my little "threesome" more than any man alive. You have made me so thrilled I could cry. Maybe I will. I won't be the same all day.

I will end this kind of short because I'm still very nervous and excited. All the guys coming off patrol will hear our good news. When my nerves settle down, I'll write a longer letter. I love you all. Send me a picture as soon as you can. More tomorrow.

All My Love to Mommy, Mike, and Cathy.

September 10, 1967
My Tho, Vietnam

Hi Sweetie, Mike, & Cathy
Now that I've settled my nerves I will try to fill you in on what little news there is. I am still thankful that all went well with you and Cathy and I look forward to seeing pictures. Please send them as soon as you can.

Yesterday, while on patrol, we caught two VC with no ID cards. One was about 20 years old and the other one about 35 or 40. We tied them up and put them on the back of the boat. Then we took them to an outpost a few miles upriver where they have a policeman stationed. Well, I wouldn't have believed it if I hadn't seen it with my own eyes. We put the two VC on the pier and waited for the policeman to come down and pick them up. He arrived about ten minutes later and asked where we found them. We told him on a water taxi a few miles from here.

Image 6.1: South Vietnamese Police Station.

He turned to the VC and asked them questions and got no answer. So, he took my M-16 rifle off my shoulder and put it on automatic and fired close to their feet. They still didn't answer, so he killed both of them right on the pier. He about cut one (the

20-year-old) in half when he shot him at such close range. My eyes about bugged out of my head. Blood flew all over every one that stood close by. What a real mess! We kicked the bodies off the pier into the river.

That's the way these people are. When I first got here, I wasn't used to seeing a lot of blood. But, I've seen more in this short time than I ever have in my life. I'm used to it now. It doesn't bother me except for when I see the wounded little kids.

By this time, you and Cathy are prob'ly home. What did Mike do when he first met her? I wish I saw his face. Is he still asking questions like he does?

I mailed his package yesterday. You may get it before you get this letter. It's a beret, a sleeve patch, and a VC flag we took off the two that got killed on the pier. Don't let Mike tear the flag up. I want it as a souvenir.

We go on a patrol at 1800 and will head down to an island to test fire our weapons. This island is loaded with VC, so the Navy has designated it as a free-fire zone. In other words, we can unload our weapons on it anytime we want to.

I may get a whole new crew tomorrow morning.

Well Sweetie, Mike, & Cathy, I will close now and get ready for patrol. I love all of you with all my heart and miss you even more than before. All I can do is picture what Cathy looks like, but I know she is just lovely. Tell Mike to take good care of her for his daddy. I will write more later.

All My Love,
Daddy

September 12, 1967
My Tho, Vietnam

Hi My Three Sweeties,
I hope you can read this as I'm lying in bed writing just before Taps. I received another letter with a picture of Cathy from you today. She is gorgeous! Most men always say a newborn baby is not pretty, but honey, she is beautiful. I love the picture and I've shown it to everyone. I can't believe she is so cute like she is at four hours old. And both of us made her possible, not just me. If

it wasn't for our love for each other and our families, the good Lord wouldn't bless us with her. I'm so proud that you're my wife, and I have such a wonderful family now. I can't wait to hold her and kiss her. That goes for you and Mike too.

I'm glad everyone thinks she is pretty, and in reading your letters I know you are just wild about her. Did Mike throw a fit when you came home with Cathy? He will watch and take good care of her I'm sure. He is just that way. I'm so lucky you and Mike and now little Cathy are in my life. I adore you for being you and bringing me two beautiful children, and above all not having any trouble during birth.

Last night on patrol, the VC attacked a hamlet on our river. They killed four people and wounded 15 others. Our two boats took out the injured. We put seven on my boat and eight on the other one. The extra weight cut our speed to about half of normal.

We started for My Tho, which was 23 miles away and we did what we could for the casualties. We had four ARVN soldiers and three civilians on my boat. One was a 21-year-old woman who married less than a year ago and she was 8-months-pregnant. She took bullets in both legs and her side. She bled to death about 10-miles away from My Tho. We tried our best to save her, but it wasn't enough.

A bullet also hit her husband in the wrist. He went to pieces when the interpreter told him his wife died.

It's a damn shame that the VC goes on killing innocent women and kids for no reason. I can't really understand it. Just before we got in, a soldier with a chest full of shrapnel died right there on the boat. And one on the other boat didn't make it.

When the pregnant one died, I couldn't help but think, here I am a new daddy, and you are safe at home with our kids, and what would I do if this ever happened to me. I would go crazy. Thank God, you're where you are.

Well love, I will close now and get some sleep. I love all three of you more each moment and can't wait to hold all of you again. Take good care of yourselves. More later.

All My Love to my three sweeties,
Daddy

September 13 - 22, 1967

It took nine days for the telegram to arrive to let me know Joyce gave birth to Cathy. The Red Cross was really slow.

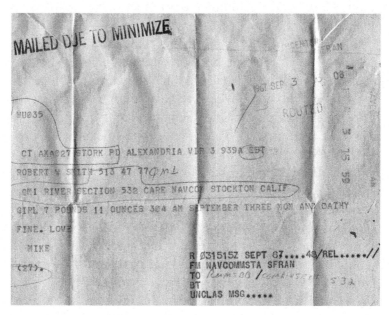

Image 6.2: Telegram I received nine days after Cathy was born. Notice who sent it to me – 3 ½ year old, Mike. Boy, did I get a kick out of that.

I hadn't written a letter in quite some time because we operated with a Navy commando unit. They trained in covert missions in the Sea, Air, and Land. They are better known as SEALs.

We took them with us on a patrol and inserted them on a small island. They went ashore to see if they could "zap Charly." For three days, we stayed in the area to support them if they needed us. Eating and sleeping on the boat wasn't our idea of a good time, but we did what we had to.

On the tower that held our radar dome was a small set of colored lights. We used different patterns of red, green, and blue to communicate with the SEALs. For example, they would flash red then blue as a signal letting us know they completed their mission. We returned the same pattern to let them know we got their message and will extract them. We pre-arranged the directions they wanted us to follow with specific patterns. It was a simple system that worked well.

Helos flew out and dropped barrels of fuel to us. The barrels weighed a lot, and we fumbled a lot to get them out of the water and aboard the boat.

The SEALs killed 13 VC during their mission, but they lost one man. We brought him back on our boat. He was shot through the groin and left side. He served in Vietnam for 17 months, and they shipped him home when we got back into My Tho.

So, you see death didn't care about your age, sex, nationality, skill-level, or training. If you made one mistake at the wrong time, you died. Sometimes, you didn't even need to make a mistake. You just had to be unlucky. Sadly, I witnessed a lot of both.

Joyce mentioned in a letter that she hoped I didn't get ideas to extend my tour. Well, she didn't have to worry about that because getting home and meeting our new daughter as soon as possible became my first priority. Hoping and praying I'd make it home in one piece was my second.

I wanted to stay home with my family and do a bunch of nothing for my 30-days of leave when I returned to the States. I knew I would be busy getting ready for my next orders, wherever they sent me. With around 300 days remaining in Vietnam the time went by fast, but all I thought about was getting home to my family.

September 23, 1967
My Tho, Vietnam

Hi Sweetie, Mike & Cathy,
As I have a day off, I thought I would get caught up on some of my letters. So far, this week has been quiet on the river. That's one trouble all the crews experience out there. When it's quiet, it's only human nature to relax and drop our guard.

That's when the VC is most likely to strike because they put a bounty on our heads of $500.00 in all the villages. They haven't collected from anyone, but they watch us from onshore all the time.

We got word today that next month we may get stationed on a Landing Ship Tank (LST) for three months. You know what an LST is don't you? We saw them tied up at Little Creek all the time. It's not the best duty as they are crowded, and they have water restriction hours on them too. All we can do is go if they send us. However, no one wants to.

Image 6.3: USS Harnett County (LST 821). Note the two PBRs tied up, and two returning from/going to patrol as well as the two helos on the ship's deck. Keep in mind that each PBR is 32 feet-long. It's a big ship!

Right now, I'm at the club writing this letter, watching a golf match. A football game comes on at 1500. No one knows which one yet, but the seats are filling up fast. That's one of the best morale builders we have here, other than mail.

I bought Mom a birthday card and sent her a letter too. I know she will be surprised to learn I can get them here.

We received intelligence that the VC was supposed to cross the river with a load of ammo and some troops. We had six boats in the general vicinity waiting to catch them, but they didn't cross. Sometimes the information is wrong and all we can do is go by what they tell us and follow orders. Maybe next time.

Yesterday we got a new man in from a PBR section at Cat Lo, a base north of here. They sent him because they accused him of being kill-crazy. He got into a firefight with the VC down at Cat Lo and was ordered to kill everything that moved. So, he did. He killed 13 people on a sampan, and they weren't VC. An officer ordered him to do this. It wasn't his fault. So, when they found they were wrong they transferred him here. He seems normal to me. I guess someone must be the scapegoat.

How is Cathy doing now? I'm anxious to see pictures of her. I will prob'ly get some soon I hope. And send some of you and Mike too. How did Mike like his beret and flag?

I will go out tomorrow morning again at 0530. I like the days as there is more activity on the river. At night, it's a little weird out there and my hearing has improved since I've been here. I listen for and react to any sound when I'm out at night.

Well love, I guess I will close now as not much is new here. More later. I love and miss all three of you very much, Kiss Mike & Cathy for me.

Bye for now.
All My Love,
Daddy

The letter above references how one of our challenges was to stay alert to danger and not get a little lazy or complacent, so to speak. During the night patrols, it was customary for two of the men to sleep while the other two stayed awake and on watch.

A few weeks earlier, I held watch on a quiet night. I had the motors off and drifted down the middle of the river with the natural flow of the current.

I felt a rhythmic rocking motion–forward, bump, backward, forward, bump, backward, forward, over and again. The gentle sound of water splashing sounded like a lullaby. The boat stopped moving and when I opened my eyes, I saw the sides of the river bank within arm's reach from our bow.

My adrenaline surged into a panic-mode because I fell asleep, as did my crew. I quickly started the engines which woke the others, and we scrambled like chickens with our heads cut off.

I sped us away from the bank and back out to the safety of the middle of the river.

Nester was the first to speak up, "Smith, you dumb shit! You fell asleep, didn't you? You know it's hard enough to stay alive out here without you trying to get us all killed!" Nester was right. He justifiably gave me a good-natured ribbing. He got his payback from the crew riding him hard about the M79 incident. I deserved the harassment from the rest of my crew too.

Thankfully, we got away from the bank without so much as a scratch. We avoided a bad situation and I'm not sure how. Sometimes we had to shoot our way out of danger, and other times we got lucky. There's no doubt good fortune was on our side because the VC wasn't in the area that night.

While we joked from a safe location, deep down, guilt swept over me because I fell asleep. My mistake could have killed my crew, an open wound that haunted me for quite some time.

Image 6.4: PBR MK II. A forward gunner is sitting in the twin fifties tub, coxswain/boat captain under canopy, and another crew member keeping eye on river bank.

Image 6.5: Crew obviously not concerned about any VC on this boat as they check IDs. No weapons in hand. Forward gunner not at-the-ready.

KIDS IN THE CROSSFIRE

October 2, 1967
My Tho, Vietnam

Hi Sweetie, Mike & Cathy,
You're prob'ly wondering what has happened by not getting any mail. Well, I've been so busy patrolling I've had no chance to write.

Would you believe in the past four days we've been in four fire fights? Last night was a real lu-lu. Our relief boats arrived, and we started back to My Tho when the VC set off a mine about ten feet in front of our boat. We were lucky they didn't hit us. However, we got a good wash down, and it scared the "H" out of us.

We turned around and made a firing run along the beach. The VC shot at us with about 100 rounds of automatic-weapon fire and about 30 rounds of semi-automatic fire, but only three bullets hit the boat. Meanwhile, the other boats made their run behind us. I called in for helo support and four came and unloaded their rockets on the river's edge.

It was really something to see with all the bullets flying. We, all the PBRs, fired 5,000 rounds of .50-caliber at the VC. We found out later that we killed 34 of an entire VC company and blew up four of their huts.

This morning, one of our boats received about 75 rounds from the bank while they patrolled a different river. So far, we haven't heard about anyone being hit. And farther down south, another river section's boat sank after three recoilless rifle shots did their damage. Three crewmen and a Vietnamese Policeman died.

The VC are acting up and we have been getting into it with them. I hope it calms down. My normal boat was being worked on again, so I was on someone else's boat. It sure seems like when I'm aboard another boat something always happens.

I hope all is ok with you and my little family. Sometimes, I miss all of you more than I can tell you, but you know I will make it all up to you when I get home.

I am sending you more pictures that I think came out well. Hopefully, you have an album now to put them all in. When I'm finished over here, we sure will need one with all the pictures I'm sending. It will be nice to show company and look at in years to come. I hope I get some of you, Mike, and Cathy soon.

We have gotten little mail. The VC are prob'ly blowing up the roads again, but I hope not. I will make this a short one and write a long one tomorrow, a day off. Excuse the writing, I'm writing while on patrol. I miss you and love you more each day. Kiss the kids for me.

Bye for now.
All My Love,
Daddy

October 3, 1967
My Tho, Vietnam

Hi Sweetie, Mike, & Cathy,
I have a day off today, so I will try to get off a few letters while I can.

I got two letters from you yesterday. One was dated 16 September. It prob'ly got lost somewhere along the way. Sweetie, never think your letters are boring. I love reading them. Keep writing the same way. I look forward to mail call like a little kid looks for Santa Claus.

I bought a nice camera last payday. It's a 35 mm Nikon, made in Japan. I will take it tomorrow with a roll of color film and will send the pictures to you as soon as I can. So, Sweetie if you want to, buy the Polaroid and take some pictures of Cathy for me.

You should have gotten the pictures of the dead VC by now. When we killed them, we didn't know where they were. We fired along the beach and just hit them. I was nervous taking the pictures.

Since I bought my camera, I make it a habit to bring it wherever we go. I will send all the pictures to you.

I'm so glad Mike loves Cathy like he does. He prob'ly does it because we loved him like that when he was as little as she is. I don't think he will change either. He isn't a mean child.

Well my three sweeties, I will close now. I love you with all my heart. Kiss Mike & Cathy for me. More later.

All My Love,
Daddy

October 12, 1967
My Tho, Vietnam

Hi Sweetie, Mike & Cathy,

Yesterday was my lucky day. I got two letters from you and pictures of our little girl. I showed everyone the pictures. Some of them twice. I put them up in my locker with the other two of Mike and you. She is a little doll. I can't wait to hold her. Kiss her and Mike for me.

I'm glad you got the gruesome pictures. They aren't nearly as bad as seeing them in person. I've seen so much blood since I've been over here, it doesn't bother me now at all. However, I will never get used to seeing the little kids get caught in the crossfire.

I took a few pictures of the girl with her arm blown off and will send them as soon as I finish the roll. I have about 10 or 12 more on the roll. They are color prints too. The two of the girl are of me bandaging her up. I hope they turn out ok.

The VC have raised hell again in this area. They fired a rocket at one of our boats yesterday but missed by about 10 yards. It went clear across the river and blew up a hut and killed an old man. The boat crew got the VC though with a grenade launcher. He won't fire anymore rockets

Image 7.1: I'm dressing what's left of a young woman's left hand. She also took a lot of shrapnel in her chest and she is leaning over with her head facing the bottom of the boat screaming in agony. Her sister is looking at the camera and covered with blood. We later took them soup and toothpaste while they were in the hospital.

If we go on the LST, we will prob'ly stay on the Ham Luong river and operate from there. That area isn't as quiet as around My Tho. We will just wait and find out later. Don't worry about me as I'm very careful. I wear my flak jacket all the time.

The reason each section has a turn on the LST is because they don't have a base camp in that area. The LST is a floating/anchored base and the men get no liberty and stay aboard for three months. It's our turn so the other section will get liberty and relax a bit. I will let you know when we are to go as soon as I find out for sure.

Image 7.2: PBRs tied up to USS Garrett County (LST 786). We'd climb up a rope ladder dangling from a boom to board the ship. Not an easy feat after a 12-hour patrol. Seawolf helicopter making approach to land on deck.

Where did Mike get it about the flag? I hope he keeps it up. Tell him his Daddy is very proud of him. He must learn quickly to already know about kids saying the Allegiance and the flag. He is a smart kid, and I hope it continues.

Tell Charlie when I get home we're going fishing. As much as I've been on the river, I'm a cinch to catch a bigger and better fish than him. Haha. We might even let the "old squirrel hunter" dog come with us.

Well baby, I will stop now and eat lunch. We go out at 1730 and I will write more soon. I adore my threesome more each passing hour. Kiss them again for me.

All My Love,
Daddy

October 15, 1967
My Tho, Vietnam

Hi Sweetie, Mike, & Cathy

As I have free time I will get off a few lines to my threesome. It has been raining here for about three full days and nights. I will go out early tomorrow, so I hope it has quieted by then. And I thought the rainy season was over with.

The mine that exploded in the water a few weeks ago was a command detonated mine. We can't see any of the mines because they are about two feet below the water. When a boat passes over, the VC manually set it off from the riverbank. If I had been right over the mine, they would have blown the boat to pieces. The other boat with us told me they saw water shoot about 100-150 feet in the air. I couldn't tell as it all happened so fast.

We were very lucky, as the VC misjudged our distance over the mine.

When we get in a firefight coming off patrol, we have at least four boats to help. We patrol in groups of twos on one river, and two other PBRs patrol the other river. Plus, four helos from the nearest Navy helicopter base are available to support us with firepower. We didn't wait long last time as it only took them 10 minutes to get to us and unload their rockets.

Image 7.3: A UH-1E "Huey" from Helicopter Attack Squadron (Light) 3, HA(L)-3, nicknamed Seawolves. Notice the narrowness of a canal versus the wide expanse of a river. We were much more susceptible to take on fire here.

As far as support goes, we don't need too much as we can fire 3,000 to 4,000 rounds from our .50-caliber in less than five minutes. I know we put the hurt on that VC company. We killed 34 and wounded about 80 or 90. A helo flew north of where it happened the next day and saw the rest of the company moving through the jungle. He fired rockets at them, but it was so dense he couldn't tell if he got any of them or not.

As of tomorrow, I will be a patrol officer in charge of both boats. They told me last night after I got in. It's a good promotion with a lot more responsibility. I won't get any more money or another rate, but it will go into my service record. Each two-boat patrol carries a patrol officer responsible for both boats. So, now I must be very careful with both boats, not like being a boat captain in charge of one.

We have seven patrol officers. Three are lieutenant junior grade (Lt. j.g.), three are boatswain's mates and me as a quartermaster for the enlisted. I will patrol with PBRs numbered 125 and 131 most of the time.

I miss you sometimes more than others. Like today. I had a day off and got to thinking and wished I could see you and the kids. Kiss them for me and tell them I love them. And you know I love you more each day.

Well Sweetie, I will close now and get some sleep as tomorrow is another day toward getting home to you. I love you.

Bye for now.
All My Love,
Daddy

I moved out of my room where I stayed with the 126 boat crew. A new first-class, who just arrived, took my place as boat captain of 126. I didn't want to leave my crew, but that's what I had to do.

I still lived on the 3rd floor of the Carter Hotel, but I moved in with two other first-class patrol officers. Cabe was a boatswain's mate, and he used to be the boat captain of PBR 123, the fastest dang boat in our section. He had family issues at home and ended up leaving Vietnam four months early. It was such a shame because he and I became best friends. I hated to see bad things happen to a good man. Guffy, my patrol officer during my 126 boat captain duty, was much younger than me. He earned the respect of everyone around because he was a good kid. I got along great with my new roommates and enjoyed the perks of the new living quarters like being more secluded, quieter, and the cooler air conditioning.

The SEALs lived on the 3rd floor too, just around the corner. They didn't fraternize much with anyone. We liked each other enough and had no problems with them, but they were an odd bunch. I certainly enjoyed working with them even though we didn't know much about them, and they showed no interest in learning about us. They were all business most of the time, but when they let loose boy, they went to town. The team we had on our floor liked to walk around naked for some reason. I don't know why, and I mean a lot!

Image 7.4: Cabe, Guffy, and Me.

October 19, 1967
My Tho, Vietnam

Hi Sweetie, Mike, & Cathy,
I have free time, so I will get a letter off. I've been busy with another SEAL team operation. We took them out for two days this time. The VC downriver had been hitting an outpost, and the SEALs went to seek-and-destroy them. They only found a few empty huts as the VC fled not long before they arrived. They left so fast they even left hot bowls of rice on the table. All in all, it was a quiet operation. If the SEALs don't kill at least one VC on an operation, they consider it a failed operation.

I'm glad you like the pictures I took with my new camera. When I finish a color roll, I will send them as soon as I can. Tell Charlie I almost didn't get that one with all those girls on the sampan. They didn't want me to get in at first. I liked that one best also. I bought the other "crazy" hat downtown, so I would have something to keep the sun out of my eyes on the river. It helps too.

Honey, if you would, search around for a college-entry exam book for me and please send it. I think you can get one at Drug Fair or Peoples. Our officer in charge (OIC) recommended three first-class and four chief petty officers to take a promotion test for warrant officer. The test is November 20, and I want to study for it and maybe I'll luck out.

I sure love and miss my little family, especially now that there are three of us. As of yesterday, I have nine months to go. The first three months went real fast for me, and I sure hope the last nine will as well.

Well baby, I will close now as it is almost time for another night-patrol. I'll write more soon. Kiss the kids for me, Sweetie and tell them their Daddy loves and misses them more each day. Bye for now.
All My Love,
Daddy

Image 7.5: Me on a sampan with some friendly Vietnamese villagers

Things were quiet on the river for a while. We received a few isolated rifle shots from the river bank here and there, but none of them ever came close to hitting us. However, I think ole Charly took shooting lessons. On October 24 he hit our radar dome and put it out of commission. We didn't fire back because we didn't want to kill any innocent people on the beach. If the shot hit any lower, things could have gone bad real fast Again, luck was on our side.

We never knew when or where shots would come from or when our turn to get hit would come. It made us terribly edgy.

October 26, 1967
My Tho, Vietnam

Hi Sweetie, Mike, & Cathy
I struck it rich today at mail call and got two letters from you. I have a day off now and will try to get caught up as I am behind a little.

Tell Mike that after his daddy gets home, and we get settled again I might get him a little puppy of his own. I know how he loves animals, especially dogs.

My promotion to patrol officer surprised me because I thought they would take someone who had been here longer, but they didn't. I feel fantastic, and so far, no one has shown any jealousy over it. Don't worry about the Navy trying to keep me over here. When my time is due to come home, I'll be on the first airplane.

About the chief petty officer's test. They will order the test next month for about eight or nine of us first-class. We will take the test in February. They may give us a week off the river to study. Our OIC doesn't believe in field promotions, so I guess I will just have to do it on my own. I will try my best, but a week isn't long to prepare, so I will try to study on my days off.

About the rain. Last night on patrol, the rain dumped on us for seven hours. We got soaked to-the-bone. We had ponchos on, but they are useless in a long drenching rain like we had.

Last night about midnight, The VC fired 37 mortar shells into downtown My Tho. Three came within 50 yards of the Carter hotel where we stay. The guys at the hotel ran around like a bunch of chickens. We're supposed to get under our beds and pull the mattress over us if we are mortared. Most of them did, but I guess a few got really shaken up. I was on the river and didn't know 'till I got in this morning. It was quite a mess. The VC "walked" their mortars right down the street. Would you believe only six people suffered minor injuries? Most of the rounds fell in the middle of the street, not in the buildings. The streets were torn up, but no other damage except a Jeep took a direct hit and got destroyed.

Well Sweetie, I will close now as it's almost chow time. I will write more tomorrow as I go out at night and will have most of the day free. I love and adore you and miss all three of you more each passing day. Tell them I love them. Kiss them too. Bye for now.

All My Love,
Daddy

October 30, 1967
My Tho, Vietnam

Hi Sweetie, Mike, and Cathy
Well, here it is Monday, and I thought I'd get a letter off before I go on patrol. We ran into some excitement on my last day-patrol on Saturday.

We got on station about 0730 and checked sampans. About 0930, we got a call on our radio that one outpost was being overrun by a full VC company (120+ men are in a company.) We were two miles upriver and took about 10 minutes to get there. The outpost wanted us to launch grenades and mortars into the VC, about 100 yards from them. Well, we had to make sure we didn't overshoot and hit the outpost. We positioned boats 125 & 131 along the river bank and fired as fast as we could load. We shot 110 grenades from the M79 and put 45 mortars into the jungle.

An Army spotter plane flew above us and directed our fire. He got so damn excited, and he couldn't even talk to us on the radio. He kept saying, "Right on the money! Keep 'em coming. Right on the money! Keep 'em coming." He must have said it twenty times.

After we ran out of mortars and grenades, he calmed down and told us he saw bodies flying. Or, I should say parts of bodies. Evidently, we hit the VC just as they stood up to charge the outpost. We killed eight of them and wounded 14. An Army helicopter fired on and killed six runners.

When the pilot gave us a status report over the radio, we jumped and screamed like little kids. We were excited about it, and we still are. That was the first time our section used mortars because they are heavy and slow our boats down a lot! The Army Infantry uses them, but I certainly believe in them now. Everyone talked about it when we got in. The officer in charge met us on the pier and shook all our hands. We proudly took it all in.

Both the 125 and 131 boats get to paint four ears a piece on their hulls to show each boat killed four VC. The ARVN routinely cut off the ears of the VC they kill. The crews went down yesterday to paint them on. However, most of the excitement has calmed down a lot.

The VC are acting up. Every day one of our patrols gets into a firefight somewhere. So far, they have only used automatic weapons, but we know they have recoilless rifles (bazookas) down here in the delta too.

Honey, can you please send me some info on the family? I need to fill in my family history statement on my application for promotion. They want the names of my relatives, birthplaces, age, when born, etc. Answer all you can when I send you the questions. This is a must-do if I want them to clear me for warrant officer. I'll write more on this later.

Well Baby I will close now and go to chow. I love you more each new hour and adore Mike and little Cathy too. Kiss them for me and tell them their daddy loves them. I'm saving a lot of kisses for you. You may get them all in one night.

Bye for now.
All My Love,
Daddy

Image 7.6: We found these two VC hiding under the floor boards of a water taxi. They refused to talk, and we brought them to a Vietnamese outpost. I'm sure they didn't live long if they didn't cooperate. In this war, morality was as muddy and cloudy as the Mekong Delta waters.

AN OPEN WOUND

November 6, 1967
My Tho, Vietnam

Hi Sweetie, Mike, & Cathy,
I just woke up after my patrol, so I will write you a letter. I haven't written sooner because we operated with the SEALs again. We left on the third and came in this morning at 0600. It wore me out, so I went straight to bed. It's 1700 now.

We, or I should say the SEALs, did well. They killed eight VC and captured a lot of papers, documents, and a few small arms. When I got back, I found out good ole Charly mortared My Tho again. This time they hit the roof of our hotel with a single round. Guess what we have up there? Our water supply tank. They blew it to pieces, so we don't have water 'till who knows when. They are working to fix it now.

I think I told you I received my books. Before I went on a night patrol the postman said I'd have a package waiting when I got in. Well, I assumed you sent me the books I asked for. The next morning, I opened a box of goodies instead. I ate everything except four cans of soup. The canned ham was delicious. Thank you and mom for sending it.

Only three of us will take the warrant officer test on the 14th of November in Saigon. All the other first-class want to wait 'till they get more experience in the fleet. Whatever that means. I've been studying every chance I can. I 'll tell you more about it later. Bye for now.
All My Love,
Daddy

November 9, 1967
My Tho, Vietnam

Hi Sweetie, Mike, & Cathy,

Well, I would have written yesterday, but we supported another SEAL operation because intelligence reports show the VC are moving again.

My patrol inserted them, but we arrived too late. Good ole Charly burned all the houses down in the village, killed the cows, pigs, and chickens and abandoned the area. They usually take their families with them when they are on the move, but they left their women and kids behind this time.

The SEALs turned the families over to the ARVNs. I can't be certain, but they likely killed them all. They are blood-thirsty bastards too and don't keep VC prisoners around after these operations. The ruthless brutality I saw when I first got here shocked the daylights out of me. I expect and see it every day now. Honey, you can't imagine how awful these people are, but I'm not lying.

Today, Charly hit a fellow in my section. The boat he was on entered a canal and the VC let him get in a little way before they open-fired. A rifle bullet from the beach hit him in the head and two struck him in the shoulder. He's only 19 and has been here just three weeks. As far as we know he is still alive but everyone in the club was in a sullen mood tonight. And to top it off, the crew didn't kill any VC either. Maybe next time.

Now for a little good news. I got two letters and a can of goodies from you today. I will prob'ly dig into it tomorrow because it all looks better than rations.

I'm glad you got the pictures I sent and will try to be in more of future ones. And speaking of my gut, I guess I'm eating well and having a few beers when I don't have to patrol the next day doesn't help. Haha. I still smoke so that's not it. Just good clean living. Haha. You can mention that to Charlie; I'm sure he'll laugh like hell.

It's a good idea that you're shopping early for Mike and Cathy. You should find some bargains. Tell Mike if all goes well his Daddy will be home next year and we'll celebrate a real Christmas then. And honey, as I won't be with you, I found this coupon in a magazine and ordered the circled items for my little sweeties. You don't need to pay for them. I already did. They should come in the mail to you. Put them under the tree from

"Daddy in Vietnam." I will feel better knowing I helped you make them happy with presents from Daddy.

Well baby, I will close and get some sleep. I am tired with no day off this week, and I must go out tomorrow morning. I love you all, and you're on my mind 100% of my time off the river. Kiss Mike and Cathy for me and tell them their Daddy loves and misses them. Bye for now.

All My Love,
Daddy

When I agreed to let Peter write this book, I knew I would need to tell the events of a day that I have tried to forget for 50 years. The memory of the worst experience in my life has never left me alone. At times, I can manage to keep my recollection quiet, but occasionally it storms to the forefront of my mind. The following story is the single and largest open wound that burdens me from my tour in Vietnam to this day.

My CO assigned my boats, #125 and #131, to a 6:00 pm patrol on the Cua Dai estuary. I believe the date was 16 November 1967. As patrol officer, I used the call sign, Coal Iron Six and headed down the My Tho river to relieve boats #123 and #139.

A more senior patrol officer gave me an order over the radio from his location on My Tho's Cua Tieu Estuary. He held rank over me as a lieutenant junior grade (we simply referred to them as JGs), but he had very little experience with the My Tho River Sections.

He directed my two boats to enter a shallow and narrow canal which left no room to make a quick escape. Our mission was to support an outpost being overrun by a whole company of 150 VC. An imminent firefight with the likelihood we'd suffer at least one casualty loomed over me. The JG ordered me into a known "hot" canal.

Now, during PBR school instructors drilled into our heads, "Never, I repeat, never enter a hot canal. Someone will die!" I advised the ranking officer about the danger of going in, and I refused his order. He threatened me with a court-martial if I didn't respect his command.

I could have spit nails because this so-called officer had no experience on the rivers. While he stayed away from trouble on the other estuary, he jeopardized my career, my life, and the lives of my crew. He infuriated me and gave me no choice but to respect his order and pray for the best.

I radioed my cover boat and told them not to follow me. Under no circumstances would I allow the VC to kill two birds with one stone. We had a few hours of daylight left when I brought #131 into the canal.

I crept in because I couldn't exactly figure the water depth and I didn't want to strand the boat high-and-dry. The 50-yard wide canal didn't give us much room to make a quick 180 either. Charly waited 'till we got in about 300 yards before they unloaded on us.

We heard shots fired from a distance. I told my crew to man their guns, and I stationed myself at the M79 grenade launcher. Tracer rounds ripped through the thick air above our heads. They have a distinct sound almost like a bumble-bee crossed with a whistle. A few seconds later the damn VC zeroed in and hit us with automatic-weapons. We "walked" right into an ambush with no place to go.

We returned fire with all our guns aimed at the river bank where the shots originated. The coxswain did his best to turn the boat around. I immediately called for helicopter support because we were sitting ducks.

Image 8.1: Helicopter Attack (Light) Squadron Three. HA(L) 3. Seawolf firing rocket to support a PBR.

We almost made it back to the main river when we got hit with a B40 rocket. The post-World War II shoulder-fired, rocket-propelled grenade (RPG) launcher weighed about 10 pounds and could disable a heavily armored tank. We sat motionless in a fiberglass boat!

An excruciating pain filled my eardrums when the rocket pierced through the port bow and exploded in front of the coxswain's flat injuring my gunner badly. The blast also set fire to the life jackets we stored in the chief's quarters beneath and forward of the twin .50s.

As I leaned over to reload the M79 grenade launcher, a second direct hit from a B40 disintegrated our radar dome. The force blew me over the starboard side.

Once I landed in the water I sank like a stone and struggled to shed my helmet and flak jacket. Although I couldn't make heads-or-tails of where I was, I somehow found the surface. I didn't feel any pain, but the loud ringing in my ears made me deaf.

From the water, I watched flames engulf my boat, but my crew continued firing their weapons except my forward gunner. I presumed he fell into the chief's quarters or on the deck. PBR 125 plucked me out near the canal entrance as I drifted toward it. They didn't know the extent of my injuries, so they laid me down on the engine cover and draped a rain poncho over me to keep me warm.

Once the helos arrived, they lit up the river bank. My old boat, #126, rescued my wounded men from the dead-in-the-water #131 which burned to the waterline. We lost all three 50s, a M-60 machine gun, the M79, all the M-16s, the grenades, all the ammo and whatever else. It was a damn shame I would never see that boat again.

Shrapnel blew the coxswain's arm to bits. My aft gunner's legs and back looked like a pincushion of metal. Both suffered critical wounds, and I didn't place much faith in my forward gunner's survival. He took the worst of the first B40 rocket, and he was a real mess.

Boat #125 headed for My Tho about 11 miles away after taking on my wounded crew from #126. Once we arrived they medevacked my forward and aft gunner out. I wasn't fatally hurt, so they loaded me back on a PBR and took me another nine miles to Dong Tam. The hospital at the 9th Infantry Army Division Headquarters checked me over.

I could barely hear, but they released me back to My Tho. People speculated about the condition of me and my crew because the CO took me off the river for three days. I tuned out all the chatter because the lingering shock stung like hell. Not knowing the fate of my boatmates ate me up. The whole incident was avoidable!

A day or so later, I talked to an officer and found the nerve to ask him about my crew. What I learned cut me real deep and has left me with an open wound and a pain you can't begin to imagine. It has never closed, never healed, and has scarred and haunted me for life.

The rocket took my forward gunner's legs clean off and killed him. He bled out—a horrific way to go. My aft gunner died too. My coxswain, well, he got a "free" trip home after they amputated his arm.

I wasn't burdened with survivor's guilt because bad things happened in a war. Crews rotated depending on the needs of a boat or a patrol, so I never developed strong bonds with most of the guys on my boat. Regardless, their deaths troubled me deeply because we all wanted to get out of Vietnam alive. They were my responsibility, and I didn't send them home in one piece. Sometimes, I could easily brush off death as just a side effect of war. But, the memory of this incident will stay with me forever. Damn that stupid-ass JG!

The supply of patrol officers in Section 532 wore very thin and my CO needed me back on the river. After only a handful of days off to recuperate from the incident, he assigned me to a patrol. Anxiety washed over me like the monsoon rains in the delta. I wasn't eager to fight the VC again, so I prayed the delta was busy but not dangerous. Concentrating on whatever my job at hand required helped me forget what happened. I focused my energy on getting home to my family and meeting Cathy. It was the only way I knew how to survive.

Word around the section traveled quickly that a big-wig sent the JG to Saigon for a general court-martial trial. I never learned the result because enlisted guys rarely receive the privilege of hearing about an officer's legal fate.

Although I told Joyce I would always share good and bad news with her, this incident was different. I survived and didn't suffer any major physical injuries, but I needed to withhold the truth from her. If I shared exactly what happened she would have worried for the next 8-months until I left Vietnam. She would greet the mailman every day hoping he'd deliver one of my letters. If I operated with the SEALs and couldn't write for a few days, she'd assume the VC killed me. I didn't want her waiting for an unfortunate-incident-letter from my commanding officer. I knew she would stare out the front window for hours looking for a gray-colored government sedan to pull in the driveway. She'd envision a uniformed military person knocking on her door to deliver "I regret to inform you..." news.

In addition, her father, Charlie, read the newspaper and watched the news every night for updates on the war. He never missed a thing related to the Vietnam. If he got word of what happened, he'd be a nervous wreck, and that would make Joyce even worse. She needed her family to be her support system, not a source of extra stress. I wanted her to believe I was healthy and safe, so she could focus on raising our children.

During my time off the river I wrote Joyce a letter and "fudged" the truth to protect her and me. I never regretted hiding the facts from her. I absolutely had to. The partially fictitious letter is below.

November 18, 1967
My Tho, Vietnam

Hi Sweetie, Mike, & Cathy,
Now that this hectic week is over, I will try to get caught up on my letters. We arrived in Saigon for the warrant officer exam on Monday the 13th at 1130. We got our physicals in the afternoon and a head "shrink" interviewed us. He said I am normal. Do you believe him? Haha. We finished up about 1700, and I hit the sack about 1900.

We stayed on-the-go for the next three days. On Tuesday, a review board of three commanders interviewed us. I don't know how I did as they didn't tell me. I had writer's cramp on Wednesday because I wrote for eight hours in all kinds of subjects. That test was the hardest I've ever taken because of the chemistry and advanced algebra. I never took those classes in high school. We finished everything on Thursday morning, and I left to come back to My Tho.

They told us if we passed the exam, we would become warrant officers for the U.S. Air Force and learn how to fly planes or helos. I guess they are short-numbered and need pilots.

The final board meets in January and the list of those who passed comes out in March. I don't feel like I made it, but at least I did my best. I'm not interested in the Air Force or being a pilot anyway, so it's fine by me if I fail. We will wait and see.

When I returned from Saigon, I had seven letters from you to read. I'm off the river today and tomorrow, so I will answer them one by one.

You must wonder why I'm not writing you, but I can't describe how busy they've kept us. I made the postman open an hour early when I got back so I could read your letters. He usually delivers mail directly to me because I earned that privilege as ranking petty officer. Oh, I prob'ly forgot to tell you I am the most senior of all 16 POs first-class. I hope you forgive me. I've been a first-class for over three years while most others only recently made their rate. The post office is often closed when I come off patrol, so the postman puts mail on my bunk in my quarters. Nice perk, huh?

I will try to tell you all that has happened since my most recent letter. My patrol last night was very "hairy."

Honey, I hope you realize I won't keep secrets from you about what happens on or off the river. We, along with 7 other PBRs, tried to prevent the VC from overrunning an outpost. We were relieving patrols a short distance from My Tho which meant we had a lot of firepower in one spot. We kept steady radio contact with our senior officer. He told me to send six boats on a firing run parallel to the bank. He sent my patrol (PBRs 131 & 125) down the canal to support the flank and we raked the area bordering the outpost. No one fired at us while going in.

The VC let us get in the canal about 300 yards. We finished blasting the borders and turned around to come out when all hell broke loose.

We received about 200 rounds of automatic-weapon fire, two B40 rockets, and a 57 mm recoilless rifle round. The B40s screamed by in front of us and landed on the opposite bank killing three civilians. The 57 mm skipped across the water, passed a few feet astern then exploded. Some shrapnel hit the aft gunner in the chest, but a flak jacket saved his life. Thank God we left the canal at full speed or the 57mm would have blown us to bits and we'd all be dead. We fired our guns on the way out, but I don't know if we got any VC. We were too busy getting the hell out of there to find out. After reaching the main river, we realized how close we came to dying, and that rattled all our nerves.

Jitters got the best of everyone and my hands shook so bad I couldn't talk on the radio or strike a match to light a cigarette. After catching our breaths on the much calmer river we settled down.

I called in the helos. They got there in about 10 minutes and blasted away with their rockets. Come to find out, we went down the canal just as 150 VC tried to overrun the outpost. Bad timing, huh? We took 12 holes in our boat from the automatic fire. They put three in our water jug, two in the flag, and the rest in the hull.

All of us said a thank-you prayer to God after we got out. It was the most terrified-of-dying I have ever been. I am not trying to frighten you, but if I held all this inside me, I would prob'ly crack up, so I'm telling you. Please don't worry about me as I try to be careful. Sometimes, I must follow orders, and do very dangerous things and I've followed them to a "T." I hope this letter doesn't scare you. I won't write about these things anymore if you don't want me to. Let me know what you think.

Well love, it seems all I did was talk about myself in this letter, but I will answer your questions in the next one. I know you miss me and I miss you and the kids more than any other man ever loved his family. We will make up for all the loneliness when I get home. Tell my sweeties I love and miss them and please kiss

both for me. I will close now and give my hand a rest. More
tonight. I love you very, very much.
  All My Love,
  Daddy
  P.S. Don't tell Mom about the canal incident.

Joyce and I visited Peter and Cathy for a long Thanksgiving weekend in November 2017. Traditionally, the ladies spend a day together, eat lunch, and buy presents for our granddogs and grandcats. I knew I'd have to share my incident on the river with Peter, so we had our day at their home and indulged in a glass of wine. We sat on a sofa and BSed a bit while I petted one of their cats that stood in my lap. I felt as comfortable as I would get.

I didn't look forward to reliving the story, but it was necessary. I only scratched the surface and avoided graphic details because I had a hard-enough time with the bare minimum. You need to understand that I've buried this memory for a long time, and I had little interest in bringing it up again. Peter kept flipping pages on a hand-sized memo pad and he seemed to shake while taking notes. My emotions overcame me, and I struggled to get the words out. Peter gave me space to compose myself and my thoughts and just sat silently next to me. During my pauses he stared out a front window with a dazed expression. I continued as best I could and Peter feverishly wrote down every word. When I finished, I told him, "I will never tell that story again and I don't want to discuss it further." His simple reply: "I understand. Thank you for sharing that with me."

We refilled our glasses and before I sat down again I handed Peter a shoe box.

"In this box are 132 letters I wrote to Joyce during my tour in Vietnam. I grouped them in order by month from beginning to the end. This is the entire story. Now, I've never shared these with anyone, but I want you to read them. All of them. I also brought a couple of books I believe will help you understand the war."

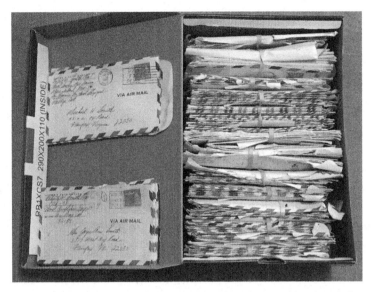

Image 8.2: The shoebox in which Joyce kept every letter (130+) I sent during my Vietnam-related time away from home. Thank God, she saved them!

He graciously accepted the letters, the books, and my wish for him to write this book.

However, there was a letter missing; the one you just read. I never wanted to tell this story again, either the real one, or the one I made up. After having a few phone conversations with Peter and hearing his passionate interest in writing my memoir, I surprised him.

Peter came to stay with Joyce and me for a long weekend in January 2018 to work on this book. For hours, we sat around a table or on a sofa and discussed everything about my tour. I showed him pictures, answered his questions and volunteered stories. Peter was fascinated the whole time.

He immersed himself in every word I spoke, and he somehow broke down a wall I had built. I retrieved the missing letter from my desk drawer and handed it to him.

Peter read it then and there and encouraged me to allow its inclusion in this book. Remarkably, he also convinced me to recount the graphic details of the incident although I vowed "Never." Over time, I grew more comfortable and am relieved to have shared the entire story with you.

I assure you, every letter that follows is factual and not fabricated.

November 18, 1967
My Tho, Vietnam

Hi Sweetie, Mike, & Cathy,
They made us paint over the "ears" on the boats for fear of the VC retaliating even more. They're already trying to kill us, so it's just as well, huh?

I will try to explain what a mortar is. We drop a projectile in a tube-like weapon that sits on deck. Imagine dropping a marble down the barrel of a shotgun, only much bigger. It is very accurate and travels almost a mile. When the shell hits, shrapnel flies in a 500-yard radius killing anything within 300 yards.

Tell Mike I love to get all his pictures and tape them up in my locker. Keep sending them. I will write him as soon as I catch up with my back mail.

Sweetie, I know you and Mike miss me and sometimes, it's hard for me to sleep because I miss you. I hate the Navy too for keeping me from you and my family for so long, but we both made this choice, and we won't back down now. You can't imagine how I feel being so far away with no one to say, "I love you" to. I try to be brave, think the best for our future, and I cry a bit too because I adore my sweeties so much. God knows how I love you. You're my whole life. Mike is too, and little Cathy makes three.

Well baby, I will write more tomorrow and send you the latest color pictures. 'Till then, I miss and love my little family more than words can say. Kiss them for me.
All My Love,
Daddy

November 19, 1967
My Tho, Vietnam

Hi Sweetie, Mike, & Cathy,
No letter from you today, but guess what? I got a Christmas box from the Ladies Auxiliary of Davis Corner. Talk about a

surprise! I thought the package was from you and Mom. It was nice of them to remember me, so I will write a thank-you note to them. They sent candy, soup, a comb, toothpaste, razor blades, a pen & pencil set and a deck of cards. I will use all of it.

About the VC bodies, the reason we dump them in the river is to show the villagers what happens if they turn into VC, and no one will bury them. It's just as well because the current takes them out to sea. Otherwise, they'd rot on land and spread disease.

I would rather wait and take a full 30-day leave than a four or five-day R & R (rest and relaxation) trip home. It wouldn't be a good morale builder for either of us when I'd have to come back. I've also become a real miser and want to stay busy and save my money.

Tell Charlie there is no such thing as a "Sunday" over here. If we are scheduled to a patrol, we go on out. Weekends are the same as weekdays, not a time for rest.

I'm glad Cathy is so cute and growing like she is. I wish I could hold her and all of you.

Things are picking up around here. Our section has had a firefight with the VC for six days straight. We know they have plenty of ammo now. They hit my old boat (#126) yesterday with rifle fire and put three holes in the shield behind the driver. Thankfully, no one got hurt.

Well love, I will close now as we have a softball game with the Army. I miss and love all of you. Kiss the kids for me and tell them their Daddy loves them. More later.

All My Love,
Daddy

November 21, 1967
My Tho, Vietnam

Hi Sweetie, Mike, & Cathy,
Just a few lines to say I miss you and think of you all every moment I can. I hope several days off the river didn't make me rusty because I have my first patrol tonight since returning from Saigon.

Are you receiving my letters ok as it's getting close to Christmas? You know what a crazy time of the year this is for mail delivery. I try to write often and I'm thankful you do too. Your letters keep me going, and they are a morale builder right now.

I am too "long" for counting days yet, but I have about 240 days to go. Do you realize this tour, when it's over, kept us separated for almost 15 months? I hope this never happens again. Maybe it will be over soon. I sure hope so anyway.

The Viet orphanage is sending 21 kids to eat a big turkey dinner with us on Thanksgiving Day. We will take care of a child and show movies for them. So, at least I'll be a daddy for a little while. I hope you all enjoy a nice holiday, but don't eat too much. Tell Charlie, especially him. Haha.

Well sweetie, I will close now and go to the exchange. I ran out of toothpaste today, so I must restock. I'll write more later.

I love you all with all my heart and miss you terribly.

Bye for now.

All My Love,

Daddy

DEAR MIKE,
THIS LETTER IS FROM YOUR DAD, WHO MISSES YOU VERY MUCH. TRY TO HELP MOMMY ALL YOU CAN AND TAKE CARE of CATHY for DADDY till He GETS Home. I LOVE YOU AND CATHY VERY MUCH AND THINK of You EACH DAY. BE A GOOD BOY for MOMMY AND DO AS SHE TEllS YOU. SEND ME SOME MORE PICTURES TO HANG UP. I THINK YOU DRAW REAL GOOD. GOODBYE NOW. I LOVE YOU.

DADDY

November 25, 1967
My Tho, Vietnam

Hi Sweetie, Mike & Cathy,
Not a day goes by I don't check with the Postman for mail,
and I usually get a letter. Hearing from my little family perks me
up, and I received two more letters today. Our mail now comes
almost every day. I don't know if they've increased our service,
or the VC has quit blowing up the roads. Whatever the reason, I
hope it continues.

We never know if the SEAL operations will be long or short.
We sleep when we can and must be in the area for fire support
when they are in the jungle. They've been going out about every
other day, but mostly at night so the VC won't see them coming.
Supporting them exhausts us most of the time.

That Mike sounds more like a Dennis the Menace each day.
He must have a good imagination and picks up what people say
around him. He doesn't miss anything does he? I hope he got my
letter ok.

Butchie must be on cloud #9 now. I'm glad he got the job
because he will make an excellent fireman. He sure did get a big
pay raise, didn't he?

On Thanksgiving night, The VC blew up Section 522's barge
(barracks) they lived on about 30 miles southwest of My Tho.
Five men are still missing. The section moved in with us 'till they
get a replacement. It is crowded here now with five guys to a
room that is built for three people. I guess we will survive.

Most of the men lost all they owned in the fire after the VC hit
them. A few of them got burned badly too. The barge just about
sank, but they saved it somehow.

Well baby I will close now and go to dinner. More later. I love
you all so very much. Kiss and hold Mike and Cathy for me.
All My Love & Kisses,
Daddy.

I couldn't ask for a better collection of sailors or soldiers to
work with than the SEALs. All of them began as Underwater
Demolition Team (UDT) members who volunteered for the

Navy's elite commando-style force. They were a rough group and didn't seem to have any moral dilemmas about killing people. Sometimes, they shot the hell out of a little hut or hamlet and created quite a ruckus. Other times, they killed their targets with only a knife and their bare hands.

I remember one operation where we picked them up at a river bank after they came out of the jungle. They proudly showed us a pair of human VC ears. They brought them back to the club and nailed them to a wall as a trophy. Well, the manager made the SEALs take them down. Most of the PBR sailors booed him. Like I've said before, some men thrived on the adventure and killing people. Not me. I know I killed my share of VC, but I never enjoyed it. I performed the duties of my job to save my ass and get home to my family in one piece.

Navy divers examined the barge wreck. They found the five missing in their racks and confirmed them as dead. The mine explosion blasted an air conditioner unit onto three of the men, and the other two likely burned to death when the nearby fuel tanks caught fire. Hopefully, they never knew what hit them.

The VC killed five PBR sailors with one mine. The club held a memorial service and every PBR sailor attended. It was a very sad day for the section and made us more determined than ever to go out on the rivers and seek revenge on ole Charly.

A HORRIBLE HOLIDAY

December 2, 1967
My Tho, Vietnam

Hi Sweetie, Mike, & Cathy,
Well, December has arrived, and I've been here almost five months. After the holidays, I hope time will pass quickly. I got two letters from you today, and they always give me something to look forward to. As I must go out early in the morning, I should catch up on writing to you.

My being senior first-class means I've been at this rate longer than the others here. I don't know if that's good or not as they may wonder why I ain't made chief yet. Haha. I have two privileges they don't. One is a reserved chair for movie night, and the other is the mail. Big deal huh!

I hope I didn't scare you in my letter about the canal incident. Knowing you understand makes me feel better in sharing these things with you. My intent is not to keep you in the dark about anything that happens here, good, or bad.

All canals are different. The one we went in was about 50 yards wide, long, and winding. We followed orders and entered a hot canal. We almost didn't come out. Whenever I think about it, chills tingle through my spine.

Well love, I will close now and take a nap. I'll answer your other letter tonight after I wake up. We have mail call about 1800 so I may get more from you. I love and miss my little family more than any man can. Kiss them all for me and tell them I love them. More later.
All My Love,
Daddy.

Now that I have taken my nap and feel refreshed, I'll write another letter to my sweeties. I checked on the mail at 1800, and I received the little Christmas tree you sent, and I must say, it is a real beauty. Thank you so much! Our room seems a bit more festive now. I also got my present from Mike and Cathy, and I hope I can wait 'till Christmas morning to open it. Haha. Let me know when they get their presents from me.

I'm glad you found a job that is close to home. The pay sounds decent and I can't wait to find out how you like it. Now, as soon as old Johnson approves our pay raises, we can save a lot of money. It won't be much of a raise, but every little bit helps. After I put away my savings, I will still have $20 a month to live on. That's plenty as there is nowhere to go and nothing to buy here.

As I finished that last line, we heard mortars hit down the street. I will continue to write 'till they get closer. Getting mortared doesn't bother us anymore; we've gotten shelled four out of seven days this week. They rattle our nerves now and then. If we're in bed, we roll over and go back to sleep if they hit far away. I've only hidden under my rack once so far. Thank God that doesn't happen often. Haha.

Well sweetie, please know that I love and miss you, Mike, and Cathy terribly and with all my heart. Kiss both for me and tell them their Daddy loves them.

Bye for now.
All My Love,
Daddy

December 8, 1967
My Tho, Vietnam

Hi Sweetie, Mike, & Cathy,
Honey, I want you to stay busy but don't work yourself into the ground. No job is worth it.

I'm glad Mike got his letter and I made him happy. I try to let him know I think of him all the time. In fact, I can't tell you how lonesome I am without all three of you.

I took care of a four-year-old orphaned girl named Mghin (pronounced Min) on Thanksgiving Day. A few months ago, the VC killed her parents when they overran her village, but she escaped into the jungle. Smart little girl. I even taught her how to use a knife and fork instead of chopsticks. She got the hang of it quickly too. I feel so badly for these kids.

I hope you have done your Christmas shopping by now as you know how crowded the stores get close to the holiday. I don't have any to do as there is absolutely nothing worth buying over here. Honey, write me and tell me what Mike and Cathy and you got for Christmas, so I can sort of celebrate with you.

Well baby, I will close and get ready for inspection (personnel in greens.) I'll write more soon. Bye for now. I love and miss my little family.

All My Love,
Daddy

December 11, 1967
My Tho, Vietnam

Hi Sweetie, Mike, & Cathy,
I got two more letters today and as usual my morale shot up again. I know I've told you about my feelings when I receive letters telling me about home. You're the best wife a man could ever want, and I can't tell you how much I love you, or what you mean to me. I thank God each day for giving me a wonderful wife and family.

As for the sailors from Section 522 who died on the barge? I only knew one of them. He was a 19-year-old Mexican boy and a gunner's mate third-class from my class at Mare Island. It's a real shame too because he was a nice fellow.

I'm glad you appreciate the toys I sent Mike and Cathy. He will prob'ly run the batteries down the first day. And I think it's a great idea about creating a doll collection for Cathy. Now is the time to start as she is so young. One thing is for sure sweetie, I'd like Cathy to be a "real girl" as much as you do because Mike is all the "boy" we can handle. I want her to grow up in pink dresses and bows like a little girl should. I can hardly wait to spoil her. You make her sound real cute in your letters, and I'm anxious to see more pictures of her.

Tell Mike, as soon as we get settled again I will buy him a dog. I hope he changes his mind about a Collie though because they can be huge dogs. I plan on getting him a puppy that won't grow up too big, and after he has it a while he will hopefully forget about Lassie. Maybe?

There hasn't been too much action on the river lately, at least nothing big. Snipers still fire at us a lot, but no real firefights. I hope it stays quiet. We get mortared about every other night, but so far, the VC haven't hit close since they blew up our water tank.

Well sweetie, I will close as it is almost time for lunch. I miss and adore all of you. Keep counting the days. Bye for now.
All My Love,
Daddy

December 12, 1967
My Tho, Vietnam

Hi Sweetie, Mike, & Cathy,

As I just got in from patrol, I thought I would get off a few lines to my sweeties. It was quiet for most of last night 'till about 0500.

We went toward the bank of the river to investigate a sampan that we heard. As soon as we turned on our spotlight, we took about 20-30 rounds of small-arms fire from the jungle. Nobody got hit, but two bullets made a complete mess of our rivers map hanging on an armor shield that protects the coxswain (boat driver). Thank God the bullets missed him! Once again, luck was on our side.

We got away fast and launched mortars and grenades into the jungle at them. The VC didn't shoot anymore, so maybe we hit them. Navy helos came after we called them and shot up the bank to "hose" down the area as we say over here.

I guess the old love bug has got Butchie. He sounds like me when I first started dating you huh? Tell him to stay single at least 'till I get home ok.

I plan on sending a few Christmas cards if I can ever find any. Everything is scarce over here. We got a few ornaments for a tree in the mess hall. I know you all at home try to cheer me up a lot, and it helps, but I'm just not in the Christmas spirit. Next year I won't be like this and we will have our best one yet.

I will make this a short one Honey as the office just called and wants to see me about something. I love and adore my little threesome more each day and miss you with all my heart. Kiss them for me. More tomorrow.
All My Love,
Daddy

December 18, 1967
My Tho, Vietnam

Hi Sweetie, Mike, & Cathy,
Just a few lines to tell you I love you and give you what little news I have to share. Not much is happening on the river as the VC has quieted for some reason. Maybe they will stay that way.

Honey, remember when I ended my last letter by saying the office wanted to see me. Well, my section (532) commanding officer and the commander in charge of both 532 and 534 (also in My Tho) met with me.

They checked my service record and needed to confirm that I passed the test for an advancement. I told them I did in August 1966. I about fell over when my CO said he will recommend me for a field promotion to chief petty officer. The idea never crossed my mind because he doesn't believe in field promotions.

They sent the recommendation letter off yesterday and if the Bureau approves, I will learn the result by February. So, cross your fingers, toes, and everything else and hope all goes well. It sure would be nice to come home as a CPO. My pay would go up about $70 or $80 or more a month. I'll be heartbroken if I don't get either warrant or chief, but we will see what happens. I wanted to wait and surprise you, but I'm so excited I can't keep this a secret.

As far as the food over here. It's not the best or the worst, but it's all we've got. On the river, we warm up sea rations (ugh) on the engine manifold. I'm so sick of them! That's why I'm always thrilled when you send a box with soup & stuff.

About Butchie. I bet he gets married before I get home because he sure seems serious enough. Has he talked to you about it yet?

Tell him he better wait 'till after 22 July, or I will really fix his ass when I see him again.

Well baby, I've run out of news, so I will close now. If I learn anything about making chief, I'll let you know, but don't be too upset if they don't promote me. We may as well quit kidding ourselves. We will both be disappointed. I love you and Mike and Cathy more each day. You're my whole life. Kiss the kids for me. Bye for now.

All My Love,
Daddy

December 24, 1967
My Tho, Vietnam

Hi Sweetie, Mike, & Cathy,
Well, it's Christmas Eve, and by the time you get this letter, the holiday will have come and gone. I know we aren't used to this, but we both realize it must be this way. I want you and the kids to enjoy as nice a time as you can without me. Next year, we will celebrate a special Christmas; it'll be one to remember.

The radio has been playing carols since around the 20th and they dressed up the mess hall and club with decorations. They are doing their best to make it seem at least a little festive. The club is having a big party tonight until 0100. However, I will miss it because I'm on patrol starting at 1700, but I'm off all day tomorrow. I would prob'ly get smashed anyway, so it's just as well.

Yesterday, the VC shocked and disgusted all of us here at My Tho. The orphans spent the day with us again and we ate another nice dinner. About 10 minutes after they left the VC hit their truck with a rifle grenade. The blast wounded almost everyone and killed three kids under 5-years old, and one of the Catholic nuns.

An American PFC (Private First-class) who drove the truck brought them back to our hotel even though the explosion wounded his shoulder. If you saw those kids, you would have cried, and a lot of our guys did. What a mess. Blood covered the whole back of the truck, and the little ones died instantly. Those who lived screamed hysterically, and we couldn't console them because they were so scared. They were just kids!

The VN Army driver of a Jeep that followed the truck high-tailed it and ran like an absolute coward after the attack. Now, you know what we're up against over here. The entire so-called Vietnamese Army is a bunch of lazy, yellow, slant-eyed sons of bitches and every one of us here feel that way. We have to prod them to do any work. They steal anything they can, and above all, they are the most scared and yellow no-good bastards alive. We've all grown to hate them!

If Charly ever attacks My Tho, we can rely on them about as much as Custer could count on jet planes. I'm sorry I sound so bitter sweetie, and you know I don't normally act like this. I guess the VC, the VN Army, and yesterday's scene with the kids makes me this way.

It sounds nice the way you've decorated the house for Christmas. I'm sure it looks pretty. Did old Santa think Mike was a real mess? Honey, I enjoy hearing about him, and we are very lucky to have a little boy like him. He is one in a million. I'm sure Cathy will be the same and I love her as much as I love you and Mike. I hope she will feel the same for me.

Let me know how Mike reacted on Christmas morning. I bet he didn't sleep a wink and I hope he left something out for Santa.

Well Sweetie, I will close now and go to dinner. Don't forget that I love you, Mike, and Cathy with all my heart and try to have a nice holiday without me. I'll do my best if you do. Next year we'll celebrate a Christmas for all to remember. I promise you. Kiss and hug the kids for me.

All My Love,
Daddy.
P.S. Merry Christmas, Sweetie

Image 9.1: They caught me off guard. Christmas morning. Obviously, we were out in the middle of the river away from any potential danger. No shirt, no flak jacket, no helmet. The VC didn't let us wear this "uniform" often. Single .50-cal machine gun over my right shoulder with the metal shield. M60 machine gun above my head not in its rightful place after cleaning. I'm sitting on the engine cover maybe getting ready to eat another disgusting sea ration.

Image 9.2: PBR crew member boarding and searching a junk boat. Man holding rifle is a Vietnamese interpreter/policeman.

HAPPY NEW YEAR?

January 1, 1968
My Tho, Vietnam

Hi Sweetie, Mike, & Cathy,
Well, the old year has gone, and the new one is here. It's good to say I'll be home this year. In fact, I have 198 days to go, and I can't wait to be less than 100.

I worked 12 hours at the club last night for the New Year's Eve party, and I'm beat because it stayed open 'till 0100. They gave me the day off today so maybe they felt sorry for me. I certainly don't mind.

Your Christmas letter arrived today, and it sounds like everyone got some nice things. You'll get my present when I step off the plane at Dulles come 22 July. Next year we will have the best Christmas of all honey because I will be home one way or another.

I bet Cathy was a real sweetie in her new outfit. I wish I could see and hold her, but it won't be long 'till I can. About Cathy's doll collection. I bought her a pretty Vietnamese doll that's wearing a dress with the country's colors, and she has coal-black hair too. I will send it home soon, so she has three now.

We are having a cookout with hamburgers, hot dogs, steak, and maybe even potato salad at the piers after the boats tie up tonight. I'll take some pictures for you. It's been awhile since I've sent any to you. I'm looking forward to getting more of Cathy and Mike and you too. Can you send some soon? I hope so.

Sweetie, we got notice a few days ago that we may move to the LST on the Ham Luong River around the 15th of January. There's no official word from Saigon, so all we can do is wait for them to send us the go ahead. Section 534 will cover the upper end and we'll patrol the lower. I'm not too sure, but when I learn more I will tell you. From what I hear though it's not the best duty in Vietnam, and the mail is bad with no service half the time.

Well love, I've run out of news, so I'll close and get some chow. I miss my little family with an ache in my heart. Come July, I will make up for all the loneliness we've gone through. Kiss the kids and tell them their Daddy loves them. Bye for now.
All My Love,
Daddy

January 5, 1968
My Tho, Vietnam

Hi Sweetie, Mike, & Cathy,
Just a few lines to tell you I love you all and miss you more each day. It has been quiet on the river lately, but we expect the VC will start their Spring Offensive any time now. So, all we can do is wait for them to make the first move.

I'm glad you approve of my part-time job. It keeps me busy on my day off as there is absolutely nothing for us to do here in My Tho. Anyway, my time here passes faster and I make an extra $25 a month which I use for my laundry and personal items. I figured out, or tried to, that I can save $1500 for sure, and maybe $1700 if I really pinch my pennies before I come home. And if you save the allotment I send you we should have quite a nest egg put away, around $3,000 for the year. Pretty good, huh? There are so many things I want to do when I return that those savings will come in handy.

I figured the news about the orphans would upset you. A few guys were friendly with the ones who got killed and they are heart-broken. Remember Mhin? Well, the only reason she didn't get hurt is because she rode up front in the cab with one of the nuns. I sure don't know what will become of those poor kids.

As far as writing to someone about them, a few guys already have, but it won't do much good. You see, the ARVN authorities are cowards, yellow, and all-around bastards. They take bribes and steal anything lying around. We, all the U.S. military in Vietnam, despise them with a passion.

We don't hate the poor villagers who work in the fields because at least they're trying to make a living. The reason we continue to fight is for the kids and the farmers who are honest and help us now and then. Sometimes, they offer helpful intelligence like where the VC are, where they are going, or how many we killed and wounded after a firefight. They do this knowing the VC will kill them if they "talk" to the enemy. So, they lose any way you look at it. And don't worry about us doing anything for them. We give them our sea rations, and they get clothing from C.A.R.E. They're in decent shape physically, but mentally, who knows.

Well baby, I'll close for now and go on patrol. I love you, Mike, and Cathy with all my heart and miss you all too. Kiss the kids for me. More later.

All My Love,
Daddy

As I mentioned in that last letter, we tried our best to support the villagers, the farmers, and the kids who were victims of the ruthless VC. But damn Johnson, Westmoreland, and all those other idiots over in Washington told the world we were winning the war against the spread of communism. They said we successfully defended the ARVN's effort to keep their independence and freedom. Well, that was all bullshit too. Sometimes, Charly threw down their arms and defected to the other side, but the VN Army deserted just as often. The TV news, radio, and papers certainly didn't report those facts. We, the Allies, weren't quitters. I'll admit many of us didn't like our jobs or missions, but we damn sure always stuck together. No way in hell we would help the enemy either. We wanted to stay alive while aiding the innocent Vietnamese people. We did what we could.

Many guys from the base collected money for the orphans after the truck episode. I took $100 downtown, a lot back then, and I spent every penny on toys. We wanted to give the children presents for their New Year's celebration called, *Tet*. The poorly-made toys broke easily, but they were all I could find in a war-torn country. The kids surely didn't mind; they were happy to get something. They knew we tried to help them even though they didn't understand the war.

The people in the city thought I was nuts for spending all that money on toys. We also gave the nuns $300 for the children's burial expenses.

I saw many of the kids after the accident and I could only hope they were doing ok. They seemed to be.

January 8, 1968
My Tho, Vietnam

Hi Sweetie, Mike, & Cathy,
I will write a quick letter to you before I go out at noon with the SEALs. My patrol will take them into a canal to blow up VC bunkers that reconnaissance planes spotted. Charly builds them as fast as we destroy them. We must stand by for who knows how long in case they need fire support from us.

A funny thing happened a few days ago. We use a loud-speaker on our boats to play recorded messages trying to persuade the VC to turn themselves in to the government. Even though the tapes are in Vietnamese, I doubt anyone listens to them. It's a dumb idea if you ask me, but orders are orders.

Well, we got in close to a river bank and played a Vietnamese tape until it ran out. Then we hit them with "hick" music: Johnny Cash, Kitty Wells, and Hank Williams. The VC let Johnny finish, but when Kitty started singing they opened fire with automatic weapons. I guess ole Charly doesn't like hillbilly music huh! Haha. They hit the speaker with three rounds, and a couple pierced our hull. It wasn't so funny then, but we can laugh now. We scurried around and fired our guns and old Kitty just kept right on singing. We laughed and laughed after we cleared the area. I wish you saw us because you would have cracked up too. We don't know if we killed any VC as we were too busy getting the hell out of there. I hope we did anyway.

Well, the official word came and we're going to the LST. We're supposed to be onboard by the 20th of January or sooner. We will prob'ly be on it for four months or more. I will be a short-timer when we come off and return to My Tho.

Honey, the mail service isn't the best on the LST, so we will just have to put up with it. If you don't receive my letters as often as you do now, please understand we can't get mail on or off the ship. The LST moves around quite a bit on the Ham Luong, so bear with the circumstances and try to make do, ok. It's just another thing out of our control.

When I go out today, it will be my sixth straight patrol. I'm tired as I didn't get one day off this week because a few guys got ear infections and couldn't patrol. I don't know what causes the infection, but many people around here have gotten sick. So far, I'm ok though.

Well sweetie, I will close now. I miss you, and I've told you how much I love my little threesome. More each day. I'll write more later. Bye for now.

All My Love,
Daddy

Although I laugh about the Kitty Wells story now, it reminds me that we never knew when our luck would run out. We prepared well for firefights even though we weren't always alert, and the war made a mess of our nerves. I don't remember where the country music came from, but it broke up the long and sometimes monotonous patrols on the river. We didn't expect the VC to shoot at us but looking back I guess we should have. I'm sure our superiors had no idea we had music tapes on the boat. They certainly would not have approved, but we had them anyway, and thankfully we escaped the area without much trouble.

We, or I should say the SEALs, obtained a lot of useful and accurate intelligence, so they kept us busy. In our pre-patrol briefings for SEAL ops we always received the order: "Bring 'em in, fire when needed, and bring 'em out. Alive!"

I will never forget a patrol where the SEALs killed six VC and captured three others. Their missions always focused on more high-profile targets than say just searching and finding a few drug smugglers hiding on a sampan. The SEALs, with the help of Vietnamese police interrogated prisoners to get information for planning other operations. Once they got what they needed, or sometimes if a prisoner wouldn't talk, the policemen killed Charly right then and there.

Well, I took one prisoner on my boat, and he immediately prayed to Buddha while repeating a phrase in Vietnamese. The interpreter said the man was "terrified of men-with-green-faces" and begged us not to kill him. I never saw a VC that scared before. I guessed the SEALs' (men-with-green-faces) reputation spread. We certainly weren't going to kill him, but I couldn't say the same thing once we delivered him to the police.

Image 10.1: Captured VC praying to Buddha.

January 12, 1968
My Tho, Vietnam

Hi Sweetie, Mike, & Cathy,
Well, here it is almost half of January gone. On the 18ᵗʰ, I will have six months left to do. Hooray! I know you're just as anxious as I am to get out of this place. The days continue to go by fast. Thank God for that. I figure the busier I stay the faster the time passes.
We haven't heard about any of the peace bids with Hanoi. They are prob'ly like the ones before if old "Johnny Bird" has anything to do with them; they've got to be messed up in some way.

Last night's patrol was routine until the VC shelled an outpost with mortars and heavy weapons, but they only wounded two soldiers. We got word over the radio to support the outpost, so we fired almost all our ammo. Ole Charly never returned fire, so I guess we overpowered them.

We headed back to My Tho for more ammo and on the way in we took fire from a river bank about five miles from base. With only 200 rounds of .50-caliber left for each gun, we couldn't stay and fight, so we shot up the rest of our rounds and went home. We called in the Seawolves and they arrived about 10 minutes later and hosed down the area.

This morning we got a report of 14 dead VC. We may have killed more, but we don't know how many bodies were tossed into the river. The helo guys credited us with seven dead, and they took credit for the other seven. We always split our confirmed casualties with them 50/50.

One of our guys asked, "Why not give them one dead and us 13?" but we couldn't do that. Sometimes we get greedy. Haha. When we're in a fight and zap a Charly or two, it's like dividing up money or something. That's the way it is. Fair is fair, right? The helos help us stay alive, and they love when we "scramble" them because action is happening somewhere, and we keep them busy.

Well sweetie, I'll make this a short one as we must go out a bit early tonight for another SEAL operation. I'll write more after I come in tomorrow. I love you and miss you and can't wait to see my little family again.

All My Love,
Daddy

Over the next two nights, our assignments put us on a hot river section we seldom patrolled because a full company of VC, or more, was always close by. Life was hard enough dealing with the fear of not knowing when we would engage Charly in a firefight. But having to go into a known hot area made everyone a lot more edgy. Our only comfort was we could escape a wide river faster than if we were stuck in a narrow canal.

Three sampans tried to cross the river, so we pursued. They saw us coming and turned back toward the riverbank. Merchant farmers knew they couldn't be on the rivers at night and they always stopped when we approached their boats. The VC avoid, retreat, and run.

When we reached the empty sampans, we towed all three into the middle of the river and dropped grenades in them. I wish I took pictures because the boats blew up like fireworks in really colorful pieces. It brightened our night, and we enjoyed a few quiet nights because we didn't get in a single firefight, which was fine by all.

On January 18, 1967, a terrible incident hit close to home for me. It ripped the "Band-Aid" from the open wound I tried to heal from that I suffered back in November.

The VC hit one of our boats with two B40 rockets and wounded the whole crew. The sight of blood and blown pieces of flesh all over the boat made me sick to my stomach. It sent me right back to reliving the moments when the VC attacked my patrol and killed two of my men with the same damn weapon. I came up to the hotel from the PBR piers and I literally shook in physical and emotional shock.

Image 10.2: Salvaged and blood-stained (lower left corner) PBR. B40 rockets create a mess. The crowd spoke little as they looked on with awe and fear.

We got word that a Vietnamese policeman, who was on the boat, died a few days later. We also learned the coxswain survived, but he lost his right arm and left eye. The other crew suffered serious but not critical injuries. I never heard what became of them, so I assumed they lived, and I'm certain they returned to the U.S.

To this day, I cannot find the right words to describe the damage that a rocket inflicts on a fiberglass PBR and to the men aboard. I still can't understand how I survived in November 1967 and I don't know how anyone lived after seeing that boat torn to pieces.

January 21, 1968
My Tho, Vietnam

Hi Sweetie, Mike, & Cathy,
I hope Mike and Cathy are over their colds now. I know you do the best you can with both, but it's difficult to watch him and her every minute. We must bear up to this separation for a little less than six months before we can be a family again. Keep thinking how much easier life will be when I get home. That's what I do, and it sure keeps me going. We're both counting the days, but if we stay busy, time will pass faster. I try to volunteer for as many patrols as I am able.

Yesterday, I received great news. About a week ago, the mission for my patrol was to mortar a VC village because they were holding a religious meeting of some sort. Well, we went in about 2300 and fired 40 mortars and 1,000 rounds of .50 cal. We got word that we killed 11 VC and seriously wounded eight, including the religious leader of the group who was the one we wanted.

All this goes in our service jackets. Since arriving in Vietnam, I've been involved with killing 28 VC and wounding 12 others. I'd like to kill every one of the bastards but there are too many of them. When we kill them, more to take their place and we are getting into more conflicts. The fighting slacks off for a while, then gets worse. I've been in-country now for over six months, and I'll be damned if I see any change!

111

If we're going to win this war, the ARVNs need to stay out of it. They mess up everything they do. Our leaders must be blind or stupid to keep telling the world how skilled the Army of South Vietnam is. You would have to see them to believe how awful they are. Well, enough of that.

Just keep this in the family as I don't want other people hearing about how fouled up it is here. I don't need anyone to cause trouble for me and the rest of us. One last remark - the big-wigs better wake up or all our young relatives will be here soon!

By the way Sweetie, I got my care package today and it feels like Christmas. I don't have to eat those damn sea rations for a few days as this will prob'ly last me awhile on the river. Thank you for the envelopes and writing paper too because they are hard to find.

Well love, I'll close now as I must go out on patrol again. Each passing day brings me closer home to you, Mike, and Cathy. I can hardly wait. I love you all so very much. Kiss the kids for me.

All My Love,
Daddy

January 23, 1968
My Tho, Vietnam

Hi Sweetie, Mike, & Cathy,
Well, another quiet patrol is over and now I have one less to pull. We got a message that said the VC will attack most of the outposts on all the rivers between the 22nd and the 24th of this month. They didn't hit any last night, but maybe they will tonight.

I got wounded while we shelled Charly near an outpost during my patrol on the 21st. Haha. Nothing serious. We moved in close to the riverbank to give our mortars their maximum range. I guess I was busy watching the bank, holding the mortar tube, and I didn't move my hand out of the way fast enough. A fin on the first shell grazed between my thumb and index finger and sliced it open. I couldn't see well because it was so dark, and I focused on bombing the VC, but I felt something sticky on my fingers. My adrenaline was pumping, and I failed to realize what happened 'till after we fired about 14 more rounds. When things calmed down, I cleaned my blood-soaked hand and bandaged it up. After I got off patrol, a corpsman put four stitches in me. Hardly worth messing with. All the guys call me, "W.I.A." - Wounded in Action. It's a big joke to them. I laugh right along with them, but I'll bet you there are more than a few officers who would want a Purple Heart. And I'm not joking.

We're supposed to go aboard the LST on Friday the 26th of this month. I will write you about the conditions after I get aboard and let you know what it's like.

A bad and unfortunate accident happened yesterday at the PBR piers. A SEAL was booby-trapping flashlights with TNT and ball bearings when something went wrong, and he blew himself to pieces, instead of Charly. What a mess! He died instantly and prob'ly didn't feel a thing. We hope so anyway.

So, you never know from one day to the next what will happen. Sweetie, hopefully you realize I don't tell you about these accidents to scare you. I need to share with you the tragedies I've seen before they take over my mind which wouldn't be good for anyone. It's no picnic over here, and I'll be glad to get out of this stinking country.

I will close now and get some sleep. I adore you and can't wait to hold all of you again. Tell the kids I miss and love them. Kiss them for me. Bye for now.

All My Love,
Daddy

I came in from the river and saw telltale signs of an awful disaster. I didn't think we received enemy fire but fresh blood covered sandbags that surrounded a hut where SEALs cleaned their weapons and fabricated explosives. The entire area was a real mess. I later learned SEAL Fraley died while inserting C-4 explosive into a booby trap. When the VC picked up a strategically-left-behind flashlight and pressed the power button on a lethal bomb exploded. No one knows for sure what went wrong but the Navy lost an incredible sailor and we lost a great man to an unfortunate accident.

Fraley was a young third-class in an aviation discipline I believe, and everyone liked him. I barely kept myself together when fellow SEAL, Rios came into the club in full uniform for one last drink before escorting his fallen friend and brother home. You know, the gray sedan with government plates pulling in front of his family's house. We all felt the pain and sorrow of yet another open wound.

Like I've said before, we didn't need to be friends with a comrade-in-arms for their death to cripple us. Not only did the VC want to kill us, but a freak accident could take our lives without warning or effort from our enemy. Fraley died from plain old bad luck. We never knew how or when it might be our turn to go home in a body bag.

The threat of dying by the hands of the VC loomed over me like a stationary dark cloud blocks the sun. Fraley's accident, on our soil, reminded everyone we didn't have a luxury of making mistakes. Death wasn't selective, prejudice, or compassionate as it seized any opportunity for success. I still had half a tour to serve in-country, and the war already inflicted enough open wounds to last me a lifetime.

About telling Joyce these stories. You must understand I couldn't talk to any of the men on the base. They would have considered me weak-minded and unfit for duty. There ain't anyone who wanted to be on a PBR boat with a thin-skinned patrol officer. I tried like hell to be a "real man" and forget about the nasty stuff I saw, but horror is hard to hide. Joyce always made me feel better because she never judged me. If I wasn't honest with her or didn't share any details, I would have felt horrible. A lot of guys closed off their families and I don't know how they kept their sanity because the war tore me up inside.

January 25, 1968
My Tho, Vietnam

Hi Sweetie, Mike, & Cathy,
Boy, I almost fell to the floor today with all the mail I got. I received three letters from you, two packs of photos, and a letter from Mom. Honey, I'm on cloud nine after seeing the pictures of little Cathy. She is without a doubt the prettiest and cutest baby in the world. She is adorable. When I get home, she will be the

same age Mike was when we returned from Guam. And he was cute then too.

I have 174 days left here which sounds a whole lot better than 365! The first 191 passed by fast and I certainly hope they continue to do so. I will be thrilled to get home to my little family.

Image 10.3: Joyce with Mike and Cathy

The fight you heard about on the news was near here but didn't involve us. It's a hot canal I've mentioned to you before, and we checked out the area two days earlier. A Riverine Force went back, and the Navy lost six men, including a commander who got hit with a 57 mm rocket. The Army also suffered several casualties on their LCMs (landing craft mechanized) and Monitors. Even though those crafts are heavily armored, they are easy targets because they are incredibly slow. They don't have the speed our PBRs have.

A lucky day for us, but not such a good one for the Riverine Force. Just one of those things I guess.

About the LST. I received word two minutes ago that we leave Monday for the "T". The USS Hunterdon County (LST 838) is not ready, so we will be on the USS Jerome County (LST 848) for a month before switching.

Well love, I will close now and write Mom. I think I owe her a letter. I love you for sending pictures of my sweeties, and I can't wait to see you all. Kiss the kids and tell them Daddy is lost without them. Tell Mike to help you and be good to his sister.

All My Love,
Daddy

Image 10.4: USS Hunterdon County (LST-838). PBR being lowered/lifted from a boom.

THE TET OFFENSIVE

Shortly after midnight on January 30, 1968 North Vietnam and the Viet Cong launched a history-making attack. The official name for the operation was The General Offensive and Uprising of Tet Mau Than 1968, but is better known as the shortened, Tet Offensive.

The NVA and VC coordinated surprise attacks in all regions of South Vietnam and targeted provincial capitals, cities, towns, villages, hamlets, military bases and outposts. They hit everywhere!

The first wave of strikes caught the Allied Forces off guard and endangered several strategic installations. Initially, the North Vietnamese achieved military success, but they suffered heavy casualties as the fighting progressed and the Allies regained control of tactical cities and towns. However, the many intense conflicts did not escape the public eye in the United States. Westmoreland led Johnson and other politicians to believe the NVA were incapable of inflicting major damage to South Vietnam and he was succeeding. Plain and simple, he was full of crap and the Tet Offensive proved him wrong! Popular support in mainland U.S.A. hit an all-time low, and the people spoke with country-wide protests.

February 2, 1968
Ham Luong River

Hi Sweetie, Mike, and Cathy,
I don't know when you will receive this letter as our mail service is bad down here. Anyway, I hope it won't take too long to reach you.

I'm sure you are watching the news and saw the VC hit all over Vietnam. I'm writing this to tell you not to be too worried as I am ok so far.

We left My Tho on the 31st of January at 0900. We travelled seven hours to reach the USS Jerome County (LST 848) which anchored about a mile south of a town called Ben Tre. After we got all our stuff aboard, we headed out on patrol. It was a quiet night until about 0400 when all hell broke loose.

The VC hit Ben Tre with two battalions (about 2,000 men). Our command sent six PBRs from 532 and two from 534 to support 30 soldiers in a nearby U.S. Army outpost.

By 0700, Charly controlled three-quarters of the town and the marketplace located only 300 yards from the outpost. The Army were about to evacuate and surrender as things looked bad. My patrol, plus two other boats entered the canal to prevent that from happening.

We received a lot of rounds from snipers on the way to the post, but nothing big. As we reached the outpost, Charly hit us with automatic weapons fire and rifle grenades. We retreated about 300 yards to get out of their range. We reloaded, started back in, and they really put it on us with more grenades and rockets. They hit the boat in front of me, wounding three out of the four crew, so we backed off again. After a cover boat took out the injured men, we tried to go in again, but the VC firepower was still too strong.

By this time, the Seawolves arrived and lit up the banks of the canal. Between us and the helos, we killed 55 VC, but that's just a drop in the bucket when you consider they started with 2,000.

We fought them from 0700 to 1000, and they kept coming at us and are still there! So far, the VC have lost 150 (killed) in Ben Tre, and Lord knows how many more are wounded.

Honey, if you saw the streets of the town, you would have gotten sick. Dead bodies were lying everywhere, and four three-story buildings burned to nothing. It was like watching a movie out of Hollywood.

And Sweetie, anyone who says he wasn't scared to death is full of you-know-what. Anyway, Thank God, we all got out alive. Well, I guess our three wounded aren't so thankful. One is in serious condition as he took a lot of shrapnel in the leg and will lose it. The other two got hit in the shoulder. At least everyone survived!

Maybe, I shouldn't tell you all this because I know you worry about me, but you would if I held a safe job over here too. I can't keep it bottled up inside me and you need to learn the truth of our situation from me and not the TV news or papers.

Things remain serious in Ben Tre. The town is 3/4 burned down because Navy jets from a carrier off shore completed several air strike missions. We're still on a Code Red but at least the outpost is better off since 300 U.S. Army arrived today.

About My Tho. The VC hit there as hard as Ben Tre and fires destroyed 3/4 of the town. They blew up the Catholic church, the orphanage, and two wings of the hospital. We don't know if the kids got out or not. I sure hope they did. The news reported My Tho and Ben Tre were hit the worst in IV Corps (southernmost geographical & military region) and that's news I do believe.

I've been here and on the "T" for three days and completed a patrol each day. The LST is crowded, but we have air conditioning and the food is excellent too. We will only be on here 'till the 17th of this month before we transfer to the Hunterdon County, which should be better. Honey, just keep using my old mailing address as PBRs pick up our mail in My Tho every couple of days.

I'll write more later as I must go out again. I love my sweeties more than anyone knows. Kiss them for me and tell them I love them and you more than ever.

Bye for now.
All My Love,
Daddy

Image 11.1 Seawolf helicopter providing close-range support to a patrol. We kept them busy and they kept us alive.

We survived the Tet Offensive, and I thanked God I reached my 32nd birthday on February 2, 1968. I didn't have the time or a festive mood for celebrating. Besides, the only gift and party I wanted was to live another a day which meant I inched closer to getting home to my family.

Life aboard the LST took some getting used to. Assigned LST crew loaded our drinking water, two cases of sea rations, 5,000 rounds of ammunition for the .50s, and boxes of grenades onto the PBRs. I counted my blessings because negotiating the boom and rope ladder just to get on and off the boats was already difficult. Never mind having to climb with cumbersome food and ammo.

While the chow tasted much better than on the base at My Tho, it wasn't always available. The unpredictability of our patrols kept us on the river and sometimes we wouldn't return to the LST on schedule. The cooks didn't care because they worked hard to clean the mess area after serving the rest of the ship. After getting shot at for 12-14 hours, we looked forward to eating a nice hot meal instead of sea rations. But, we'd come in and only find a few bologna sandwiches and a carton of milk left out for us. We felt disrespected which didn't sit well with me or my crew as you can imagine. I remember that I requested to meet with the captain on my scheduled day off the river. The two of us discussed the problem, and he agreed we deserved better. He assured me the cook would prepare a real meal for late-arriving boats, even if someone needed to wake him out of bed. I felt damn proud for sticking up for men, and they thanked me too. We never ate another bologna sandwich while in Vietnam.

The LSTs operated as a floating and mobile base. They pulled anchor and moved at least twice in a 12-hour period to prevent the VC from attaching mines or explosives to the hull. When underway for a short trip, it cruised about five knots per hour and typically dragged the PBRs alongside. However, if we needed to travel a long distance, the booms lifted the boats out of the water and stored them onboard in the decks below. This allowed the ship to reach its destination much faster.

Image 11.2: USS Garrett County (LST 786). A "scrambled" Seawolf returns to the landing deck.

February 5, 1968
Ham Luong River

Hi Sweetie, Mike, & Cathy,
I know how worried you must be with all the fighting now. Well, on the river it's at least a little calmer than our first couple of days here.
There are still plenty of VC in the area, but they've been quiet the last three days. We remain on alert 'till we run them out or kill them all. The news is reporting, as of noon today, the Allies killed over 17,000 VC, and the numbers keep climbing.
It's been ten days since we received any mail. I guess Saigon is messed up again, or the VC blew up all the roads during Tet. I understand it is not your fault Sweetie, and I'll let you know as soon as I get a letter from you. All the fighting delays everything.
I'm settled on the LST as are most of the other guys, and I can't believe I will say this, but the chow is great. Oh, and we all appreciate the air conditioning too. Our laundry gets done once a week. Not like My Tho, huh? I'm sure we will make do. Now that we're all comfortable on this ship, we must transfer to the Hunterdon County. It's supposed to relieve the Jerome on the 17th of this month as I guess their one-year tour is up.
Today four new men arrived in our section. We all kidded them about how long they will be here. I have 164 days left and I bet you are you counting too. Honey, I think about you and the kids constantly which keeps me going. Staying busy as much as I can makes time goes by quicker. Otherwise, it just drags. I guess it's the same with you huh?
Kiss the kids for me and tell them their daddy loves them and their mommy very, very, much. Bye for now.
All My Love,
Daddy

February 7, 1968
Ham Luong River

Hi Sweetie, Mike, & Cathy,

Yesterday I really hit it rich. I received six letters from you, one from my sister Barb, and birthday cards it seems from everyone. Getting mail makes me feel that my time here is worth the trouble and it puts me on cloud nine. You can prob'ly tell in my writing I don't sound very cheerful when I don't get mail.

I also got back pictures which I am sending you of the boat hit by the B40 rockets. They're not pretty but are factual. We face this each time we go on a patrol. I'm sure you realize this and worry, but it must be this way. I could hide all this from you, but you seem to want to know what goes on over here. All I can say is keep praying and maybe things will work out ok for all of us.

It's no bed of roses here, especially since the VC are active again. We get in at least two firefights a day on the river with them. All we're hoping for is we kill them or hurt them so bad that they will leave us alone.

Yesterday I went in the canal at Ben Tre where we fought our big battle, and I counted 17 VC bodies bloated and floating in the water. I took out four wounded Army men from the fighting in town. We got in and out quickly because they shot at us the whole time. Charly didn't hit us, and we were lucky. I feel sorry for the other 26 Americans still in the compound. Two VC companies are lying-in-wait and hiding in their bunkers. Even air strikes won't budge them because they are too well-protected in their tunnels. 300 soldiers from the Army's 9th Division are going in today to see if they can dislodge them. I hope they do as the compound is in danger of being overtaken.

You would think the VC would run out of men. So far, the Allies killed 280 in Ben Tre and I wish it was 2,800. Try not to worry because we have plenty of ammo and we are killing them left and right, but they keep coming. I don't know where in the world they are getting them all.

Bear with me while I catch up on my back letters as I patrol every day now with this mess going on. I'm sure you heard the VC hit My Tho. They burned down about 3/4 of the buildings and went to the orphanage and killed 23 of the kids. I won't tell you how they died because it made me sick and I'll spare you the details. Thankfully, we left before they destroyed the town.

I'm glad you replaced the car muffler. At least it wasn't anything too serious to fix and I guess it was due, huh? If we can afford it, I want to keep the yellow car for you and maybe buy a new one too. I hope we do all the things I would like when I get home. We'll see.

Cathy is such a little doll and I wish I could see her and hold her. Thank you for always telling me she is doing well. I can't wait to spoil her too, like I do with you and Mike. It's just my nature I guess.

Well, baby I will close now and go to chow. I hope I have a quiet patrol tonight. It's been a while since the river's been calm. Tell the kids I love them and miss them more than ever. And you know how much I need and love you. Bye for now. More later.

All My Love,
Daddy

You may notice in this letter how abruptly I changed subjects. In one paragraph I shared the orphanage story and was so disgusted that I couldn't or didn't want to describe how the kids died. But, in the next few sentences I talked about Joyce getting a new muffler for her car.

In reading these letters again, I often wonder how I turned off an emotional switch like I did.

You must understand seeing blood and horror over there was an everyday occurrence, and we simply got used to it. Nothing ever surprised us except a VC ambush, but we grew numb to grotesque things that would shock any civilian.

We forced our thoughts and feelings to the edges of our minds as an act of self-preservation. If we let bad things tear us up, we'd lose our pin point focus of staying alive. Otherwise, somebody would kick our dead body into the river, or pack us into a zippered black bag to go home.

Nobody wanted that, so we tried to live as normal as possible. I don't know how the guys who didn't write to their families or have good relationships at home stayed focused and sharp.

Every man in Vietnam went half-crazy trying to stay alive and in one piece. Constantly living with the fear of getting blown up and wondering, *Is today my unlucky day?* took a toll on me. You can't possibly understand the damage being in that position for months on end causes to all the senses of a man. My open wounds lingered 24 hours a day because war didn't let them heal and always burdens me with new pain.

February 9, 1968
Ham Luong River

Hi Sweetie, Mike, & Cathy,
My patrols down here are not much different from those in My Tho. Four on, then a day off unless they call us in for special ops which happens now and again. So, I'm not working any harder. The more I volunteer the faster time will pass. As of today, I've completed 136 12-hour patrols, not counting the SEAL missions. I should be well over 200 when I finish my tour.

I don't man the guns much. My station is operating the radio, calling in the air strikes, artillery, or whatever the case may be. If we get hit by small arms or automatic weapons, we can handle it ourselves. If the VC hit us with anything bigger, we call in the big stuff, like the Seawolves.

As for being brave. Most of the time, we've just been plain lucky and catch the VC with their "pants down." When they shoot at us, our mission is to get the hell out the fastest way we can. We fire every weapon and hope we kill a few before we leave, and so far, I guess we've done well. When we are stuck in an intense firefight, we're too busy to be scared. We only see the VC's muzzle flashes and hear the bullets pass by. But, after we escape, and our adrenaline settles our nerves shake like crazy. It's only human nature.

As for the fighting here, it's no different and Charly is raising hell again. The Allies have killed 267,000 or more NVA and VC but they keep coming. It's a wonder we don't run out of bullets. Thankfully, we are well-stocked. Most of this week we've really shot up the jungles from the river supporting outposts as one or two get hit daily. My section has been on the "T" for 10 days and been involved in 16 firefights. Some were small, but most were pretty good ones. I hope we killed 20,000 of the little slant-eyed bastards. We all hate them almost as much as we can't stand the cowardly ARVNs and that's plenty.

Well sweetie, I will close now and write to Mom. Kiss Mike and Cathy for their daddy and tell them I miss them and love them very, very, much. I love you more each passing day. Soon I will hold all of you again. Lord willing. More later.

All My Love,
Daddy

February 15, 1968
Ham Luong River

Hi Sweetie, Mike, & Cathy,

I hope you received my letters saying we left My Tho before all this mess started. As far as my section is concerned, we jumped from the frying pan and into the fire. I told you about Ben Tre. It got hit just as hard as My Tho and the VC are still in the area, but they are not as active. I'm sure it won't last long, and you will worry until you hear that I'm alright, but you must know by now.

Yesterday, three VC tried to cross the river. It seems they told an old lady and a small boy to take them across, or they would kill them. They held on to the side of the boat while in the water so the PBRs wouldn't see them. Well, they just about reached the bank and one of our boats spotted them. Charly got out of the river and ran. Naturally, the PBR opened fire and killed the two men at the water's edge, but the woman escaped into the jungle. They fired a rifle grenade in the bushes and that took care of her.

A Vietnamese interpreter traveled with the PBR and they sent him to get the body. They found she was a 12-year-old girl with a belt of grenades tied around her waist. You see, the VC use everyone they can for their cause and that's why I hate them so much.

I asked the boat crew how they felt about killing a young girl, and they said it was either her or them. Which is true! They took the grenades off her but didn't find weapons on the men. They threw the bodies in the river to show people what could happen if they are or turn VC. I guess it's psychological warfare. Maybe it makes sense.

Well sweetie, I will close now and write mom. I'm a letter behind to her. I love you more each passing day and the kids too. Kiss them for me and tell them their daddy is always thinking about them. Three more days and another month passed with only five more to go. More later.

All My Love,
Daddy

11.3: Vietnamese interpreter and policeman who patrolled with us.

February 23, 1968
Ham Luong River

Hi Sweetie, Mike, & Cathy,
Now that I'm two letters behind, I guess I better catch up. I've been busy as we've been patrolling daily with no time off. So far, I don't mind, but it grinds on me after a while. The VC are on the move again, so we must increase the number of our patrols. They are also trying to cross more in the daytime than at night.

Three days ago, a sampan carrying four men and one woman tried to evade being searched. They got halfway across the river before they turned around. We followed them and fired warning shots, our well-known signal for them to stop, but they kept on going. So, we fired our 50s right at them before they reached the bank. The men swam about 20 yards to shore but bullets hit the woman in the chest, pierced through her neck and sliced her head clean off. We found it lying on the motor when we came alongside. What a mess! One of the VC made it to land and ran before the 50s amputated a leg. A couple pulls on the trigger of a .38 pistol trigger took care of him as he crawled trying to escape. The other three men were still in the water and we gave them a chance to come out, but they wanted no part of us. We threw grenades at them and when the smoke cleared we didn't see them anymore. I suppose we got them too.

All of them wore red VC arm bands. We retrieved the sampan which drifted to the bank, attached a grappling hook, and pulled the mess into the middle of the river. Nobody fired at us from the beach at all. The woman's body was still in the boat but with all the bullet holes it was sinking fast. One of our guys jumped aboard and held up the severed head like a trophy while another guy took his picture. Isn't that awful?

I almost got sick, but they seemed to enjoy themselves. I realize I sometimes must kill the VC, but it's only to keep myself alive, not because I'm looking for entertainment. After that, the sampan sunk. All in all, we survived an active day.

Cathy must be growing fast. I bet she looks cute up in her high chair and I can't wait to see her. Mike wants her to grow up quickly, so he can play with her, doesn't he?

Honey, be sure to tell me when you receive the $550 check I sent. I am concerned about it arriving ok.

Well sweetie, I'll close here. I love and miss all my little family. Kiss them for me and tell them I won't be long now. More later.

All My Love,
Daddy

February 27, 1968
Ham Luong River

Hi Sweetie, Mike, & Cathy,

Just a few lines to say hello and tell you the river has been calm the past few days. I like it better this way, but I'm sure Charly won't keep quiet too long.

A letter from you arrived two days ago, and this break is my first chance to answer because we've been patrolling one after another. You know I try to write back quickly because you look for mail as much as I do, huh?

Now sweetie, I have (I hope) good news for you. Yesterday we got a message in from Saigon with the list of men who will advance. They recommended 165 Navy for field promotion from all of Vietnam. Anyway, they cut it down to 57. The decision makers awarded advancement to only three people from each river section. In 532, they are a gunner's mate third-class, a yeoman third-class, and guess who? Me!

The word isn't official yet; it should be when the test results come back from others taking the exam. If approved, I will make chief on the 16th of March or April. I'm not sure yet. I can hardly wait 'till I get a letter from the Bureau.

It sure will be nice to come home in kackie-colored uniforms instead of whites. I know you are happy for me too. I am about to bust. As soon as I receive the official word, I'll write you. I plan to send you my first set of chief's collar devices as you have stuck by and helped me. And I love you so much. It's about time we got a good break, huh? Anyway, until I hear from Saigon we must keep our fingers crossed ok? I don't want to hatch my chickens before they are laid, but that's the latest update. Are you excited as I am? I can barely write this letter.

Well sweetie, I'm nervous as a cat now, so I'll make this a short one. I'll write more tomorrow night. I've worked hard for this, so it must come through! I love you and the kids with all my heart.

All My Love,
Daddy

Image 11.4: Safe in the middle of the river. I'm on the aft .50-cal machine gun. The M79 grenade launcher is mounted atop the gun. Notice the "organ grinder" crank handle which fed a belt of grenades into the open hole next to the crank handle.

ANYONE FOR SCRABBLE?

March 3, 1968
Ham Luong River

Hi Sweetie, Mike, & Cathy,

I have a day off today, so I will write a letter to my sweeties. The river is still quiet, and I hope it remains as such for a while. I've been shot at long enough over here. A few new guys are looking for their first firefight and they will prob'ly find it when and where they least expect too. Anyway, that's usually the case.

I'm glad you think the same way as I do about the Vietnamese and their age. A 12-year-old girl can pull a trigger as fast as a 20-year-old man. Over here it's either you or them. If I just arrived, I would feel sorry for the girl we killed, but I've been in-country a while. I learned early on to hate anyone with slanted eyes and I don't trust them, especially after seeing how the ARVN work. You'd be surprised how much this war has changed me; I don't have any remorse for that young girl.

Thank you for the crossword puzzles and the playing cards you sent. They will be a big help to pass the time. When we're not on patrol, all we do is play games and read or write letters. We can also watch a TV in our room, but the reception is terrible. I guess we're too far from Saigon, so sometimes we catch a movie they show each night.

Earlier today, a chief interviewed me and took down my full name, service number, and other information. When I asked him why he needed it he wouldn't tell me. But, he said they have big plans for me soon. Someone knows something that I don't. So, all I can do is nervously wait for an official letter about my advancement. My officer in charge and everyone else seem to know the result, but they're not talking. Aren't they awful? We must cross our fingers and I'll keep you informed.

Well baby, as I volunteered to help paint our new office, I will end now. I adore you and can't express what you all mean to me.

I can hardly wait 'till I return home. Kiss the kids for me. More later.

All My Love,
Daddy

MARCH. 3, 1968
HAM LOUNG RIVER

DEAR MIKE,

I KNOW YOU CAN'T READ THIS LETTER NOW, BUT MAYBE YOUR MOM CAN TELL YOU WHAT IT SAYS. IT SAYS MANY THINGS THAT I FEEL BUT CANNOT SAY AS I AM TO FAR AWAY TO DO SO. I WANT YOU TO KNOW THAT I LOVE YOU AND MISS YOU VERY MUCH. AND I REALIZE THAT IT HAS BEEN A VERY LONG TIME SINCE YOU AND I HAVE ROMPED AND PLAYED TOGETHER. BUT I AM HERE WHERE I AM, SO THAT SOME DAY MAYBE YOU WONT HAVE TO LEAVE YOUR HOME AND DO WHAT IS ASKED OF ME NOW. THERE ARE LOTS OF LITTLE BOYS HERE THAT ARE NOT AS LUCKY AS YOU, TO HAVE A MOMMY AND DADDY AND A COUNTRY AS GRAND AS OURS. SO I WANT YOU TO BE A GOOD BOY AND HELP YOUR MOM TILL I CAN COME HOME AGAIN. REMEMBER, I THINK OF YOU ALL THE TIME AND WILL COME HOME TO ALL OF YOU SOON.

LOVE

YOUR DAD

March 6, 1968
Ham Luong River

Hi Sweetie, Mike, & Cathy,
Something messed up the mail as I got six letters from you today with two postmarked 15 Feb 1968. I think they were sent to Nha Bay by error as that's what's stamped across the back. I've never lost a letter for three weeks. Maybe all is ok now. I also received an envelope of just pictures and Honey, they are great. Seeing photos of my little family sure picks me up. They came out fine. I love them, and I feel so good knowing I have three sweeties to come home to.

Now that I'm six letters behind, I will try to answer all your questions in the right order, but I've got my work cut out for me.

Speaking of prayers. Honey, I'm like you. I know they help as I've used them occasionally over here and plan to do so 'till I'm home. I can't predict what happens out on the river. Just today, the VC attacked the section covering the upper Ham Luong (we cover the lower). Two B40 rockets hit a PBR while they checked sampans near a U.S. compound in Ben Tre. One glanced off the stern but didn't explode and the second struck directly on the aft .50-cal machine gun. It killed the gunner and wounded the patrol officer, and coxswain. So, don't stop praying. I haven't.

Looks like our little girl is growing with teeth and all. I bet she will really bite when a few more come in. Watch your fingers!

I don't think I have changed too much mentally, but I need to break a few habits before I return home. One is listening for the slightest sounds, and the other is looking for something strange. Being on the river makes me reactive to every and all noise. I duck even when we shoot the guns on the boat I am on. We abide by a strict rule while on the river. Always announce when you will fire a weapon and never fire behind anybody because that's the fastest way to get killed by your own men. So far, we've not broken the commandment. Everyone is trigger-happy and jumpy when we're out on patrol. So, a first mistake could be my last or someone else's.

Tell Mike I'm very proud of him for learning the Pledge of Allegiance. However, I would be really homesick and depressed if you sent me a tape of him saying it. I get that way now and then and I'd rather hear him in person after I come home so I can hug and kiss him when he is done. I hope you understand what I mean.

Well baby, I'm bushed tonight as I just got in a few hours ago. We've been checking an average of 800 people a day this week. As you can see, the VC are getting ready again. I'll write more tomorrow night. Kiss Mike and Cathy for me and tell them Daddy misses and loves them. I adore you.

All My Love,
Daddy

March 8, 1968
Ham Luong River

Hi Sweetie, Mike, and Cathy,
I'm glad you took Mike to the movies and enjoyed yourself. Please get out once in a while and relax. Did he enjoy it?

I can't get over Cathy being able to say bye-bye. Can a baby talk at that young age? I don't know much about little babies and can't remember when Mike said his first word. Anyway, I bet she's a real sweetie and doll just like my other two. Seeing her in person and holding her will be a dream come true.

Tell Mike I enjoy his drawings very much, and he should send them more often. We don't have a lot of storage space, so I can't hang on to them or your letters. But, I always keep important papers like the telegram about Cathy's arrival, your first letter about her and of course pictures. I live out of a locker that I must share with two other first-class. Hopefully, you don't mind me not keeping all you send because it's something I can't help, and I hardly have room enough for my clothes.

Anyway, tell Mike I show all the guys on the boat how well he can draw and write. I give the little Vietnamese kids his pictures because they are so poor, and they really enjoy them. Do you think he will understand?

I realize I haven't been home much for you and Mike. No one understands more than me, and honey it gets harder and harder to say goodbye when I leave. I hope I can get over this, but it's just my nature I guess. Thinking back on all the time I spent away from my little family really upsets me. So, I try to be extra good to Mike and you when I am home. It's rough at times because I love you all so much, but I wouldn't change a thing.

Since the time you picked me up at Tops, these have been a happy seven years. Haha. I knew that would get you! Anyway, tell Mike I will take him, you, and Cathy everywhere we go after I'm home.

I hope Cathy is over crying when she meets people by the time I return. Remember Mike did the same thing when we came in from Guam, but he got over it, and I'm sure she will too.

Well sweetie, I will close and get some sleep. I am off tomorrow, so I can write more later. I love you very much and miss you more each day. Kiss the kids for me and tell them I miss them. Bye for now.

All My Love,
Daddy

The Delta was quiet for about three weeks and nobody understood why or complained. We assumed the VC were re-arming and gathering to hit somewhere, but we didn't know for sure.

Every now and again, we'd receive sniper fire from a specific section of the river. We nicknamed it "The home of one-clip Charly." He would shoot at someone at least once a day until he ran out of bullets before retreating to his bunker. He was like a next-door neighbor you wave to each morning on your way to work. Except he wanted to kill us but always failed. He shot from too far away, so the rounds never reached. We didn't worry too much about him.

While the river was quiet, we appreciated the down time to decompress and relax, even though we knew the VC could flare up at any moment.

Image 12.1: We always made sure our weapons were clean and functioning.
Nothing worse than having a jammed-up rifle when you're in a firefight.

Besides reading and writing letters, I valued spending time with my best friend, Cabe. Believe it or not, we became good friends with our executive officer (XO). Lt. Parker frequently invited us to play Scrabble with him, but enlisted men weren't allowed in an officer's quarters. So, he'd bring a table and chairs into the passageway. Well, there's not much room in a ship to begin with, so whenever an officer needed to pass, Lt. Parker moved the whole setup into his quarters. We appreciated the temporary diversion from living in a war, and Cabe and I relished getting under the skin of our XO. We were damn good at our jobs on the river. But, we were also well-skilled in defending our choice of words and arguing for our points.

Of course, you'd never find a dictionary aboard the ship, so challenges didn't exist. Half of our fun was pleading our case over a silly word like JORE.

"Smith, what in the devil's name is that? Use it in a sentence."

"Okay. Cabe get JORE ass out on the river and bring JORE boat back in one piece."

Lt. Parker would laugh like hell. "You've got to be kidding me. Where do you come up with these words? Fair enough. You two are ridiculous! I sure hope you are as quick-on-your-feet while on patrol."

"Yes, sir. You better believe I am."

We made the best of a bad situation and having an officer around that we liked and admired certainly helped. I still have a great respect for Lt. Parker because he was cut from the same cloth as Lt. Dennis.

I didn't see our commanding officer for about two weeks as he took R & R (rest-and-relaxation) in Hong Kong. When he returned, he immediately left on a 30-day leave because he extended his tour for six months. I thought he was sick in the head, and rumors surfaced he was having family trouble at home, but no one knew for sure. War destroyed lives in a variety of ways.

I couldn't understand why anyone, including Paul Cagle, my old forward gunner, signed on to stay an extra minute in that God-forsaken place. Why would anybody put their lives on the line for another six months? Fifty percent of the men in our section extended. Paul agreed to at least two, maybe three additional tours. He paid a heavy price though, earning three Purple Heart awards and rightfully so.

You couldn't get me to extend for anything. Not for the Vietnamese people and certainly not for the politicians. Not for anyone. I longed to get home and wanted my little family to reward me with their love. That was the only decoration I wanted to be awarded.

March 29, 1968
Ham Luong River

Hi Sweetie, Mike, & Cathy,
Yesterday, a VC turned himself in to a PBR, but not mine. He gave them the location of hidden arms and ammo. At 0300 they called me back to the "T" from my patrol. I picked up the VC traitor and the SEAL team before we left to steal the VC's weapons.

We arrived in the area about 0430 under a new moon phase which kept the light pitch-black. Six PBRs went out for the operation, and we traveled up a narrow canal for three miles. We got in ok and dropped off the SEALs and the VC. We waited close by for a couple hours to take them back out.

By this time, daylight was breaking. There we sat, perfect targets for Charly if they wanted to open fire on us. Anyway, a couple SEALs brought two sampans out of the brush loaded with weapons, arms, and four VC they killed with knives. After we searched the bodies, we tossed them in the canal. We put the loot in the PBR and waited for more to come out. And it kept on coming!

Here is a small list of what we got: 22 water mines, 43 claymore mines, two M-1 rifles, two German machine guns, six boxes of hand grenades, two 75 mm recoilless rifles, three boxes of rockets for the 75s, and much more. It's one of the biggest hauls ever uncovered in the delta.

Coming out of the canal, we received rifle fire from the banks. With all those mines sitting up on the bow, it's a wonder we didn't get blown to smithereens, but we got in and out without a scratch. Thank God! We were real lucky too as a lot of VC occupied the area. I guess praying helped this time.

We are on cloud nine because our section pulled off the operation. Newspaper reporters and photographers from each military branch are all over the place and the "T" is busy with activity and excitement. Navy explosive experts defused the mines. We now get a case of whiskey and the SEALs get one too, but we must wait 'till we return to My Tho.

It looks like the VC are active again as we got into a fight with them during my last day patrol. They fired about 25 rounds at us while we checked a water taxi. They killed a 50-year-old lady before we pulled away. We returned fire, but I don't know if we hit them because the jungle is thick on those banks. More importantly, we escaped without getting hurt. I can't say the same for the woman, but oh well. The VC just don't care who they kill.

Well sweetie, I'll make this a short one and write more tomorrow night after patrol. Kiss the kids for me and tell them I love them. Bye for now. More later.

All My Love,
Daddy

Image 12.2: If these all-volunteer helo crews relaxed, they deserved it. They helped us immensely no matter the time of day or night. Notice the empty rocket rack. I'm guessing they just returned from "hosing" down the VC.

Image 12.3: HA(L) -3 Huey lighting up a VC post with machine gun and rocket fire.

JOINING THE ELITE

April 3,1968
Ham Luong River

Hi Sweetie, Mike, & Cathy,

I'm sorry I didn't write for a few days as we have been busy. We came off a day shift, and all but finished eating before they sent us out again.

Charly is really ticked off because we stole all his arms and ammo. In the last three days, we've been in five firefights with them. Yesterday, they attacked my patrol from both sides of the river at once, and a bullet went clear through the windshield of my cover boat. They missed my boat somehow, but they sure came close! The VC also hit a PBR from a different patrol (but was with us) with a rifle grenade and put a big hole in the bow. The forward gunner took a lot of shrapnel in his neck

We fired about 2,000 rounds of .50-caliber at them, but they kept shooting, so we called in the Seawolves. They unloaded all their rockets and the damn VC still didn't quit. River Section 534 sent boats from upriver to support us. They hosed the area with their guns, and that did the job. Charly stopped firing.

Today they found eight dead and 13 wounded VC, and two dead civilians. We prob'ly killed more but who knows how many ended up in the river. The report also stated the VC kept a full company (120+ men) in there. They took the 13 survivors as prisoners to Ben Tre for a little VN justice if you know what I mean.

After that incident, we returned to our normal patrols and boarded a big junk boat. A woman wouldn't let anyone search her, so we used force, and she fought like a tiger. We tied her arms together and then she kicked the hell out of us. We accidentally tore her clothes and we could not believe what we saw. She was smuggling medicine. She taped units of Penicillin, Terramyacin, and other assorted pills all over her body. She wore enough medicine to take care of a whole battalion of VC. It's no wonder she fought like a caged animal.

We took her to the ship, and an interpreter questioned her. She tried to convince us that she was selling the drugs on the Black Market in Saigon. She lied. We knew she was supporting troops and now ole' Charly will really be mad. He's been trying everything, and we always seem to catch him with his pants down.

Image 13.1: Woman who smuggled medicine for the VC by taping it to her body beneath her clothes.

My R & R request came back yesterday approved for the 20th of April. If I don't receive word about making chief by the 18th, I'll cancel my plans. The only reason I'm taking this break is to buy new uniforms. The ship gives me a clothing allowance rather than waiting for Saigon to send money. $300 won't go far, even in Hong Kong, so I'll prob'ly get more in the States. I'm still nervous as ever and you will be the first to hear if they advance me.

Well baby, I'll close now but will write you another letter this afternoon as I go out again tonight. I miss and love you and the kids very much. Only 106 days left. Thank God! Kiss the kids for me. Bye for now.

All My Love,
Daddy

April 11, 1968
Ham Luong River

Hi Sweetie, Mike, & Cathy,

Well, the news must be close. About 1230 pm yesterday, a helo came in from Saigon with advancement results for those on the LST. Many people made their rates. Three took the test for chief but didn't make it. One already bought his uniforms because he was so confident he passed. He failed, so I don't know what he will do with them now.

When I found out the rates were here for others, I figured mine is not far away. They sent a boat up to My Tho today, and maybe they will bring back my results. I hope I hear something soon because I couldn't sleep at all last night. I eventually fell asleep around 0430 this morning. It's a wonder I'm not sick with an ulcer. You are prob'ly the same, huh? If I don't find out today, we need to be patient as they only go to Saigon from My Tho once a week. Keep your fingers crossed. I'm so nervous I can hardly write, and I sure didn't expect the news would shake me up this way. I never want to wait like this again for anything. It may work out well in the end, but it isn't physically right now.

As I can't write too much more due to my nervous condition, I will make this a short one. More tomorrow. I miss all of you so much. Kiss the kids for me. I love you.

All My Love,
Daddy

April 14, 1968
Ham Luong River

Hi Sweetie, Mike, & Cathy,

As this will be my last letter for a while, I better inform you what's going on. Yesterday, we found out we are heading up north for about 3-4 weeks to operate south of Da Nang. The LST is taking us and we'll stay there 'till we finish. We will support the Koreans, who are planning a big operation. I hope it's not a long trip, but we never can tell.

Anyway, we don't expect any incoming or outgoing mail. So, you may not hear from me for a while, but at least you'll know why.

I'm sure you will worry but try not to because I am always extra careful. Please bear with it. Today is our last outgoing service 'till who knows when. If the helos came with us, we'd have no problems, but we will operate with jet support most of the time instead.

Still no word on chief. I've just about stopped guessing when I'll receive an official letter. If it's meant to be, it will happen. I can't wait to tell you the good news whenever I find out. I need to think positive.

Tell Mike when I come home we will have good times. All of us. Cathy and Mommy too. Won't be long now; about 95 days left to go.

I bet all those riots and burnings going on at home after they killed Martin Luther King are making a real mess. They do no good and I don't know when they will end, but I'm thankful you're out in Fairfax away from all that. We've talked about the news on the ship, but that's all we can do. I hope they calm down soon.

Don't let this letter shake you up, but I bet it does anyway. We need to patrol an area where no PBRs have been and will contend with regular North Vietnamese troops. They are better-trained and equipped than the local VC. I will write you every chance I can, but you may not get mail for a while after this one. Try not to worry.

As today is Easter, I plan to attend the church service. Don't faint! In fact, the whole section is going.

Well baby, I'll close now. I love and miss you, Mike, and Cathy. Kiss the kids for me. More soon.

All My Love,
Daddy

April 24, 1968
Quin Nhon, Vietnam

Hi Sweetie, Mike, & Cathy,
Well, we've waited a long time for the results and the agony is over. I learned yesterday that I officially became a chief on the 16th of April. You can't imagine how thrilled I am right now. I'm ready to pop, and I know you're happy too. Thank God!

We were on a special op, so we received all our mail just yesterday. Ten days passed before they delivered or sent anything. I was on the river and didn't get the word 'till I got back in. I let out one of the loudest yells ever recorded in Vietnam. Can you believe it? I won't calm down 'till who knows when and you're prob'ly the same, huh? I'll send you my first set of collar emblems as soon as possible. Put them away as a memento. Okay?

The mailman also delivered four letters from you yesterday and I will answer all of them eventually. Please add the picture I am sending you to our collection.

Did I tell you they canceled my R & R because of this big operation? I plan to go in the first part of May to buy my new uniforms! They are conducting an initiation ceremony this Friday the 26th at one of the clubs I guess. My nerves haven't settled yet because I don't know what to expect. Anyway, I hope I'll make it okay.

This operation we're on is a real mess. Most of the time our boats get stuck on a sandbar as the water is so shallow. So far, the Koreans killed 165 VC. Pretty good, huh? Nobody knows how much longer we will be here, but I guess we'll find out on an as needed basis.

Well baby, I'll close here as I'm still in shock, and I can't settle down. More tomorrow after I get in. I love you and the kids and miss you too. Kiss them for me. Bye for now. More later.
All My Love,
Daddy

I recall seven or eight chief petty officers and a few senior Army soldiers escorted me into the Enlisted Men's Club. I never earned the privilege to enter a CPO club, so I didn't know the rules and etiquette. Nobody told me to take off my black beret when I walked through the door which I quickly learned was a big no-no.

The bartender rang a gigantic bell three times, and it scared me half to death before he announced, "The next round is on the new chief!"

Well, I instantly made new friends when I shelled out my wallet to buy drinks for everyone in the bar. That was just the beginning of it all.

During a "serious" ceremony, a chief read a list of charges against me for which they found me guilty.

Charge I : Violation of the Uniform Code of Military Justice, Article 91

Specification In that QM1 SMITH did, three days prior to being notified that he had been selected to participate in this trail, made the statement that there wasn't NO Chief in this here Navy that he sweated and also stated in the Special Forces Club that most chiefs he has met were a bunch of flunkies.

Charge II : Violation of the Uniform Code of Military Justice, Article 134

Specification On 23 April when notified that he had made E-7 he went on liberty in the uniform of a Petty Officer First Class.

Charge III : Violation of the Uniform Code of Military Justice, Article

Specification: Disregard for Tradition, On 23 April when SMITH was told he made E-7 instead of presenting himself to the Mess President for instructions he proceeded to the club at Market Time Base and got himself drunk, and upon returning to the ship he blamed his condition on the Mess President.

Charge IV : Violation of the Uniform Code of Military Justice, Article

Specification Attempted Bribery, Upon entering the CPO Quarters SMITH was not satisfied with the bunk assigned him, he suggested that since he was a new member of the Mess that one of his fellow QMC's (one from his Section) should give up his bunk to him. (Note, fine working airconditioning)

Charge V : Violation of the Uniform Code of Military Justice, Article

Specification Adverse Remarks Towards Another CPO, SMITH made the statement that now he was E-7, he wouldn't have to take all the crap from the Officers, and he could mouth-off just like Chief JONES does and get away with it.

Well, they teased me pretty good I suppose. They forced me to strip off my clothes and wear nothing but a diaper. I took drink orders for the chiefs who escorted me, paid for them at the bar, and brought them back to the tables.

They accused me of messing up their drinks, so they made me lie on the floor, and guzzle from a full pitcher of raw eggs. I handled it well and didn't throw up. Oh, but they weren't done hazing me.

Another chief entered the room without wearing a shirt, and he slathered axel grease all over the biggest belly I ever saw on a Navy man.

He demanded that I kiss his belly button. When I got close, he put his hands over my ears and squeezed my head like he was holding a watermelon. Then, he rubbed my face all over his fat gut and the grease. It was disgusting, and that almost made me vomit!

Boy, did everyone laugh. All in all, a bunch of guys just blew off steam and enjoyed some good-natured fun.

Making chief petty officer was a special occasion for me because they are so well-respected. Sometimes, people treat chiefs better than higher ranking commissioned officers. I felt recognized and appreciated for my dedication to the U.S. Navy and becoming a member of an elite group made me proud.

Joyce stayed with me every step of the way and I will forever be grateful for her love and support. Missing the births of my children (two open wounds) and putting my life at risk every day filled my heart with guilt. I placed tremendous pressure on myself to stay alive for my family. A Navy career wasn't always easy for me, Joyce, Mike, or Cathy, but I'd do it all over again. As I've said before, I willingly and proudly served the Navy and my country.

April 27, 1968
Qui Nhon, Vietnam

Hi Sweetie, Mike, & Cathy,
They initiated me last night and I'm now an official chief petty officer. I will never forget that proud and happy day.

They put me on "trial" and ordered me to pay a found-guilty fine of $70.00 which paid for all the booze and chow. We all got smashed after the so-called ceremony and everyone had a ball.

35 chiefs attended with me being the only boot chief (newest and most junior. They razzed me real good, but I survived. It's one of the happiest moments of my life, besides marrying you.

Anyway, I'm relieved the waiting is over and I bet you're glad too. I hope we never wait that long for anything important again. Write and tell me your reaction soon okay?

We finished in Qui Nhon last night. It turned out to be a good operation for our side. Between the PBRs and Koreans, we killed 284 NVA (North Vietnamese Army), 108 VC, and captured 84 VC. We lost 10 Koreans and one U.S. soldier. Not a bad ratio, huh?

Our boats got really torn up with bullet holes and only one of us took a bit of shrapnel in the leg. We are all lucky and thankful for getting out alive without too much damage with all the fighting we did. I can't believe I am saying this, but we look forward to patrolling the quieter Ham Luong again. We should be back on the 29th or 30th.

Mail call came just once, and I know I'm behind in responding to you. We'll be on our old river soon, so I will have a lot of free time to catch up. I hope you weren't upset about us going north. It's over and we're out of that mess.

Well sweetie, I will close now. Did you get any letters from me? I will worry 'till I hear from you. Don't forget that I love you and the kids very much and miss you terribly. More later.

All My Love,
Daddy

NEW SET OF ORDERS

Wednesday -
May 1, 1968

Hi Sweetie & Daddy, & "Chief"
What else can I say now
except that I love you, I'm so
proud of you and CONGRATULATIONS!
I always knew you deserved
it and now it has paid off. It's
too bad we always seem to be
apart on occasions which mean so
much to each of us. I know you
are really happy, and Honey,
you have reason to be now. I
hope your initiation was such
that you enjoyed it and didn't
end up with a too sour head.
I know you were numb when
you made First Class but Chief —
I can't imagine what you would
be like. We will celebrate your
new rank when you come home.
In my "visions" of your return, I
have you in Chief clothes so now
it will be for real when I see
you. I don't know why but I

I couldn't picture you in the
white sailor suit. Just think - the
end of the white hat. I can hardly
believe it.

I must confess to you though that
I found out on 15 April that you
made Chief. I hope you don't
mind but I couldn't stand to
wait much longer so my friend
at work got her husband to go
through his channels and he found
out for me. He said for one not to
write you until you told me as
it may be a let down to you, knowing
I found out first. Anyway, the
letter I sent with a P.S. in short
hand was my congratulations to
you as I couldn't keep it a secret.

Even though I heard you made
Chief it didn't mean so much to
me knowing you weren't aware of
it yet. Now, I'm very excited over
it and really believe it.

Cackie sends her congratulations
and said "We are real proud of
you".

2

I think your Mom was close to tears when I told her your news. She is just as proud of you as I am.

I guess you know how my Dad feels as much as he has hoped to see you as Chief. He is just so pleased with you as if you were his own son.

Well, I will cut this short and answer the remainder of your letter tomorrow night.

Can't begin to say I love you enough and please be so careful for us and take good care of yourself.

We love you dearly and miss you so very much. Cathy and Mike send so much love and kisses too.

Our Love
Your Three Sweetie

P.S. How does it feel to be called Chief?

May 4, 1968
Ham Luong River

Hi Sweetie, Mike, & Cathy,
We are back on the old river and started our normal patrols again. I better get off a quick letter to catch up on my writing to you.
Sweetie, I'm glad you went ahead with getting your wig. I bet it's pretty and you deserve to treat yourself. Will you wear it when you meet me at the airport? I hope so.
We hear very little news about the peace talks. We all hope something will come of them, but no one has any faith in old Johnnybird. Maybe he'll fool everyone.
I received good news today. They are giving us a raise in July. My pay per month right now is $413 but will increase to $444. Not bad, huh?
Well Sweetie, I'll close and get some sleep. I adore you and my little family. Kiss the kids and tell them I love them. Bye for now. More tomorrow.
All My Love,
Daddy

May 5, 1968
Ham Luong River

Hi Sweetie, Mike, & Cathy,
The VC started up again. They hit a lot of airfields all over Vietnam last night. As it's almost Ho Chi Minh's birthday, they are gathering again for another offensive. We're expecting a big fight with them real soon. All the outposts are on Red Alert now.
The section that covered our area while we helped the Koreans got into it a few days before we returned. The VC tore up three of our boats badly, one took five rocket hits. Surprisingly, no one was killed but eight suffered serious wounds. So, you can see we never know when the little bastards will strike. I hate them all with a passion and I'll be glad to get out of this stinking country. You prob'ly feel the same as I do.

Well baby, I'll close now as I must go out on patrol soon. I have two night-patrols then four day-patrols staring me in the face.

I love you very much, and I miss you. Kiss the kids for me and tell them I love them. More later.

All My Love,
Daddy

May 8, 1968
Ham Luong River

Hi Sweetie, Mike, & Cathy,

Well, I got another letter from you today dated the 22nd of April. Apparently, the mail is still messed up because the last one I received was stamped on the 29th. Maybe I'll get the missing mail soon. I hope so.

I know how you felt with being down and depressed while I worked with the Koreans. But it's over, and we're back on our old river. Your spirits should be better now with my good news from my recent letters.

I still can't get used to being addressed as Chief Smith. I sure like the sounds of it and I'm anxious to hear your reaction. Were you a mess when Mom called you? I bet so, and I wish I saw your face.

Nothing major has started yet with the VC, but I know they will break loose soon. Everybody is tired of fighting and the more we kill them the more take their place. I just don't see or feel like we're making any difference at all. We keep doing our job and try our best to make it home in one piece. Maybe this war will end someday. I hope so.

In your letter, you mentioned Da Nang. Well, we didn't go there; we ended up farther south in Qui Nhon. They only sent our section, and we stayed 12 days while operating in a large bay behind the city. Our boats spent more time stuck aground in the shallow water than actually patrolling. It was hellish because the VC shot at us and we couldn't move. We fought while sitting still, but I think we did pretty good.

General Westmoreland sent us a nice letter and a Korean General wrote a note too. The Koreans are fantastic; they fight like no other army.

Don't mention this to anyone outside the family, but they take no prisoners. They captured around 84 VC but only held 20 for a short time. Know what I mean? I'm an eyewitness to this and I'll tell you all about it when I get home.

I wish I saw the look on Mike's face when you took him to the circus. I'm sure he enjoyed himself, huh?

You prob'ly got the letter by now telling you I couldn't send your surprise. I wanted to give you a dozen roses for Mother's Day and I am sorry, but the mail is so fouled up over here. Nothing I could do about it. I bet you were disappointed after you rushed home? You are so wonderful, and I love you so much more for being that way. Even if you did "pick me up" in a drive in. Haha. And what's this about you getting even with me in July? You wouldn't pick on a shattered war-veteran, would you? Knowing you, I guess you would, but I'll have a punishment for you too when I get home. What a way to get punished. Wow, wow, wow.

Well love, I'll close now. I adore you more than I can say. I love the kids too and miss you all so much. Tell Mike to be good for his daddy. Bye for now. I'll write more soon.
All My Love,
Daddy

The Korean soldiers tortured their captives and took no mercy. I saw them hang a VC soldier from a tree while they interrogated him. They cut off one of his legs with a machete while he dangled from a big branch. Of course, he didn't live much longer.

We heard multiple stories of them throwing prisoners out of helicopters when they would not answer questions. I don't think it mattered if they answered or not, almost every captured VC got killed by the Koreans. Thank goodness they were on our side. We didn't mind helping them because we knew they wouldn't run out on us like the coward ARVNs.

May 12, 1968
Ham Luong River

Hi Sweetie, Mike, & Cathy,
I lucked out yesterday with three letters and I showed all the other guys the card you sent too. The mail seems straightened out and maybe you are receiving mine just fine.
I'm glad Pat and Butchie asked Mike to be in the wedding. Do you think he'll behave? Our little boy will be about four and a half and I bet he's gonna look real handsome in a tux. Can you get one small enough for him? I hope so.
It sounds like a big wedding with six attendants. I'm happy Butchie thinks of me the way he does, and you know the feeling is mutual. I hope I don't let him down.
With all the nice things I've heard about Pat I can't wait to meet her. She seems to be family already and I'm sure I will like her. She's good for Butchie, huh? He is level-headed and picked a swell girl didn't he.
The VC are acting up again, but so far, only on my days off. I hope they quiet down until after July. By then, maybe the peace talks will halt this mess over here.
Well sweetie, I'll close now and eat chow as I'm on the river again tonight, but more patrols means time passes faster. I love and miss you and the kids more each day as I inch closer to coming home. Kiss them for me and tell them their daddy loves them. I'll write more soon.
All My Love,
Daddy

May 21, 1968
Ham Luong River

Hi Sweetie, Mike, & Cathy,
Today was a lucky mail day for me. I received two letters from you and I got a new set of orders.
Would you believe we might be snow-bound for most of next winter? My orders read, and I quote: "The U.S.S. Albany (CG 10) out of Boston, Massachusetts." Brrr. cold! I think we can

keep each other warm. The Albany is a guided missile cruiser homeported in Boston.

I know we want to move back to Norfolk, but like always, the Navy is in control. Baby, it's not as bad as you think, and please don't be too disappointed. We will be fine after we settle in. At least I hope I will convince you of that. Many of the chiefs on the ship here tell me Boston is a real nice place to live. Not right in the city, but in the suburbs.

We both want to buy a house in Norfolk, but we may need to put our plans off for a while. I hope you are not "pissed off" about my orders. They are Bureau-controlled, which means I have no control over their decision. If you want, I can request the Bureau to change them after I get home. Not sure they'll listen or even care, but it's worth a shot.

I report to Norfolk on the 16th of August 1968 for three weeks of career-counseling training. Do you remember when I attended this school before? Well, I guess the Navy feels I need a refresher. My new primary job will be as a Career Counselor. Anyway, it's a "racket" I'm sure I can handle. I will graduate on the 6th of September about 1000.

So, I can attend Butchie's big wedding. I won't want to miss that. Well, after I finish the training they will send me to core-commissioning school for the U.S.S. Albany. The ship is decommissioned in the shipyard and undergoing renovations. It will prob'ly go on a shake-down cruise before starting operations in January 1969. I plan to write and find out their op-schedule from August until January, so they can fill me in on details I don't know yet.

That is the whole story; I told you everything and I am anxious to get your reaction and hear what you think. Tell Mike he can still have his collie (Lassie) dog.

While writing this letter, my executive officer informed me that my R & R is approved for 1 June. The only place not booked is Penang, Malaysia. I guess I'll look for uniforms there. If not, I can always buy them when I'm home.

Well, I rattled on tonight, so I will close now as I must go out early tomorrow. I adore you all more than I can write in this letter. Kiss Mike and Cathy and tell them I miss them very much.

And most of all I love you more than any man ever loved a woman. More later.

All My Love,
Daddy

May 25, 1968
Ham Luong River

Hi Sweetie, Mike, and Cathy,

Boy, am I tired. We finished a two-day special operation with the SEALs and I am glad it's over. We helped out just once after we dropped them off in the "boonies." The VC left about 20 men behind as a rear guard, and they put up a good fight for a while. We came in and fired mortars to support the SEALs. We killed six VC, and they broke off contact and retreated. The next day the SEALs fought them again and killed 11 more. So, all in all, we got 17 of the little bastards.

We got a new boatswain's mate first-class today. Our section will lose about half its men come June and July. Many of them extended so they are due a 30-day leave which leaves us really short-handed. Saigon hasn't bothered with replacements as far as I know. They keep messing around and only have half a section, but that's their worry not mine.

Well sweetie, I will close now as it is late. I love and miss you and the kids with each passing day. Bye for now. More later.

All my love,
Daddy

Image 14.1: Most likely thinking about home. I'm not armed-and-ready for a firefight although I am wearing a flak jacket.

SHORT-TIMER'S SYNDROME

My time left in-country was real short and I didn't want to jeopardize getting home alive. So, I took five days of R & R in Penang, Malaysia on June 1, 1968. I figured I should take advantage of every opportunity to get off the river. If I wasn't on patrol, nobody shot at me, and my chances of leaving Vietnam in one piece improved drastically. I also bought chief uniforms, at a great bargain, in the clothing shop of a grand hotel where I stayed.

I treated myself to a nice steak dinner one night and a table of five Australians noticed I sat by myself, so they invited me to join them. We enjoyed each other's company while we ate, drank, and traded stories. I learned they were tank soldiers who would return to Vietnam two days later, but thankfully, I avoided the war with three more days of R & R.

I connected with them again the following day for sight-seeing, dinner, and more drinks. After our meal they brought me to a temple and told me to sit quietly on the ice-cold stone floor to respect the rituals. I saw 15-20 long black snakes wriggle toward us. They wound around my arms and neck, and slithered up my pant legs to warm themselves, but they didn't bother me. Well, I remembered I don't like snakes, so I stood up and frantically took the critters off me. When I ran out of the temple, the Aussies laughed like hell. I guess all the alcohol made me a little adventurous, or crazy. They were a good group of guys that I enjoyed relaxing with. They invited me to ride along in their tanks if I found my way to Pleiku Air Base. It would never happen, but it was a nice gesture anyway. I always wondered what became of them and if they survived Vietnam. I sure hope so.

When I got back from R & R, I visited the sick bay for a physical and vaccination shots. I gained 12 pounds while in Malaysia because I didn't eat those disgusting sea rations all the time. Although I enjoyed myself, something still bothered me.

I didn't know Joyce's feelings about my orders to Boston. She set her heart on moving back to Norfolk, VA and I wanted to move there too. But, after spending a year away from her and the kids, I didn't care where the Navy sent me. As long as they took me out of Vietnam I would be thrilled.

I received a letter from Joyce, and she calmed my anxiety because she felt as I did; she just wanted our family together again. Her parents, on the other hand, weren't as excited. I assumed they liked having her and the grand kids home with them which I understood. Norfolk isn't far from Fairfax so visiting a few times a year could be easy, but Boston was a different story.

My initial orders required me to stay in Vietnam until July 23, 1968. Between details, the Navy granted 30 days leave to a sailor and allowed more time off for transit from station to station. However, my new orders dictated that I arrive in Norfolk, VA by August 16, 1968 which didn't give me the full time off. The Navy shocked and thrilled me when they approved my early exit from Vietnam to receive the entire leave due to me.

The last time I boarded a PBR was May 31st, so I was happy to patrol again because time passed by much faster when I worked.

After my R and R, I realized being on the river for well over 200 patrols made me extremely jittery. As a short-timer, I tried hard to keep my boats out of trouble and harm's way. A handful of my crew always wanted action and firefights, but I saw enough of all that.

An incident I'll never forget reinforced the devastating toll war inflicted on me. I can laugh now, but it also hit home that the violence in Vietnam affected everyone.

I brought our boat to a stop on a bank, and we sat in one spot for quite a while. My plan, as I explained to my crew, was to ambush Charly as he came down the river.

We manned our stations and stayed alert to any activity around. A dense cover of palm trees provided a perfect camouflage for us to hide beneath. A calming peacefulness filled the thick summer air, but we couldn't relax because we'd be easy targets for the VC.

It was eerily quiet. Too quiet.

Snap.

BALOOOP.

Let me tell you, we unloaded nearly every bullet. I mean we screamed and yelled and blasted whatever enemy lie in the water.

We didn't receive return fire, so we stopped shooting.

The forward gunner shouted, "It's a damn coconut!"

Lt. Parker was right about me being quick-on-my-feet. I responded to my gunner. "Must have been one of those sniper coconuts. Son of a bitch scared us all half to death, but we got it, didn't we boys?"

"Damn Smith! You got a bad case of Short-timer's Syndrome, man. You're falling apart! And get us the hell out of here, so the real VC don't blow us to pieces."

As we created quite a ruckus, we retreated to the middle of the river and laughed and poked fun at each other. We argued over who shot first. Of course, they all chose me, so I guess I won.

My crew wasn't kidding. I lived with fear constantly and responded with panic to every sound. The slightest noise made me jump out of my skin, so to speak.

I could handle seeing all the blood and dead bodies because I grew used to all that. The VC got active and hit a merchant ship and a Viet Navy ship with rockets. Four people died, and we took 16 wounded to Dong Tam for treatment. I could deal with military men or adult civilian casualties, but not children.

Getting shot at, and the anxiety of not knowing when we would take on fire wore on a lot of guys. I didn't understand why so many wanted to extend their tours or get off the boats and go into the jungle looking for trouble. It made no sense to me.

June 15, 1968
My Tho, Vietnam

Hi Sweetie, Mike, and Cathy,
Well, half of June is gone, and I have 19 days left in-country. This has been a long year, but can you believe it's almost over?

I've only been on three patrols since getting back to My Tho with my first one being on the 10th. Next week I patrol five out of seven days, but at least the time will go by faster this way.

I received my Father's-day cards yesterday, and I liked them all. Tell Mike he does well in signing his name.

I'm sorry to hear about Bobby Kennedy and his family. They sure have bad luck. I sometimes wonder if I'm safer over here than at home with all the nuts running around.

Still no word from Saigon on replacements. It looks like I may stay on the river until I leave. I hope not as I need a few days to pack before getting on a plane out of here.

I will prob'ly fly on Pan American into Clark Airforce Base in the Philippines before arriving in Hawaii. No matter the time, I'll call you when I can, ok?

Before I come home, I need three more shots which isn't so bad. They gave me a few after my R & R in Malaysia and I wasn't sore after those, so I should be fine.

Sweetie, please thank Cackie and Bill for the nice card they sent me for my advancement. I will keep it in my scrapbook. Also, thank Karen (Coway-ann) for her invitation to her graduation. I would like to attend, but you know I can't. Maybe I'll be around when she graduates college. I hope so.

Not much going on here in My Tho with the VC although we fight with them on the river now and then. I hope they stay quiet for the rest of my time as I'm on edge more and more with each patrol. Any sound startles me, but I guess that's what happens after a long tour in war. My nerves can't hold up much longer and I know I'm being overly cautious, but I want to leave here in one piece. Flying out of Vietnam is all I think about lately.

We receive mail four times a week now which is great. I hope yours is getting to you alright. We won't need to write soon. Thank God for that!

Well sweetie, I'll close now as there isn't much new. I love you and the kids and can't wait to hold you again. Kiss them for me. Bye for now. More later.

All My Love,
Daddy

While the river was quiet, I went on what I thought and hoped was my last SEAL operation. Now those guys always lived to seek-and-destroy as General Westmoreland demanded, but I wanted no part of fighting anymore. With only a couple weeks left in-country I prayed for my safe arrival home. I never knew what trouble the SEALs would bring, and we took them out for two days, but it seemed longer. At least, I returned in one piece.

About the third week of June I learned the fate of PBR Class 33 Commanding Officer, Lt. Dennis. As a patrol officer aboard PBR 750 in River Section 535, his boats engaged in a serious firefight along a bank near My Tho. The VC ambushed them from the jungle and hit #750 with two B40 rockets and immediately killed Lt. Dennis and Boat Captain Ford. The other crew members jumped off the boat to escape the flames, but the VC shot and killed the after gunner in the water.

I can't explain how the death of Lt. Dennis affected me. You know, it was one of those "Nice guys always die" situations. He proved himself and earned my respect way back in PBR Class 33. As an officer, he patrolled the rivers as much as any enlisted man and never shirked from responsibility. He didn't go looking for trouble, but he dedicated himself to his country, to the Navy, and to his crew.

Losing him left a gaping open wound in me and all of us on the river. We were almost home with just a few patrols remaining! Lt. Dennis gave every ounce of himself to all that he did. It was a damn shame, but war is unpredictable, merciless, and heartbreaking.

While I mourned his death, I also looked forward to returning home.

June 25, 1968
My Tho, Vietnam

Hi Sweetie, Mike, and Cathy,
I got two letters from you today, and I'd better get busy answering them.
We took the SEALs out around midnight yesterday. They went into the jungle to find a 52-year-old woman who threw a grenade

in a transport jeep a few days ago. She killed one U.S. serviceman, four ARVNs, and seven kids. Anyway, we dropped them off and an hour later they came back with her. The SEALs didn't run into trouble as they killed three VC guards with knives instead of guns to prevent unwanted attention. I'm happy to say that was my last op with them.

I only have four more patrols left, two days and two nights. I can't wait to get off the river. My tension and anxiety are getting worse. I jump at any noise at all. If someone strikes a match, I know about it, but all short-timers are that way they say. I don't guess I'm any different.

So far, no replacements in sight. If no one comes by the end of this week, "sorry about that." They will just have to do without 'till someone gets here. I'm permitted to leave regardless if they send anyone to relieve me.

As of today, I only have nine days to go. These last ten crawled at a snail's pace. I guess because all I think about is coming home. Six of us leave My Tho on the 2nd or 3rd of July, and an officer is trying to get us out of Saigon for the 4th.

Well sweetie, I will close and go to chow. I love and miss you with all my heart. Kiss Mike and Cathy for me. Bye for now. More later.

All My Love,
Daddy

June 25, 1968
My Tho, Vietnam

Hi Sweetie, Mike, and Cathy,
I have good news for you. The flight list came in today and guess what? When I saw my name on the sheet, I really let out a howl. I'm so excited I can hardly stand it. Won't be long now!

I leave My Tho on the 2nd of July, one week from today and will stay at a Navy Billet in Saigon until Friday the 5th. I'm not taking any chances and will only leave my room to eat chow.

A plane departs Saigon at 1020 am and arrives 17 hours later in San Francisco. I should land in the good ole U.S.A. about 0600 *or 0700 on the 5th. So, I'll be on home soil before I left Vietnam. Pretty neat, huh?*

I guess your boss was sorry to see you turn in your resignation. Honey, you do a fine job in all the places you work and that's why they hate to lose you. What did I do to deserve a wife like you? I don't know, but I love you for all you do and all you are. You're really my sweetie and always will be.

Thank you for buying me civilian clothes as I only have two pair of slacks and four shirts and that won't be enough. Try to find kackie pants or jeans to knock around in too. I bet mom wants help with home-related odd jobs, so I'll need clothes for that. I'm sure you will fix me up ok.

Is Mike excited? I know you are and maybe Cathy too. It seems like a dream I'll finally be home soon. You may need to pinch me when I step off that plane in Dulles.

Well baby, I will close now as I must go on a day patrol tomorrow. Six more days left in My Tho and only nine 'till I leave this damn country. I adore all of you with all my heart and can't wait to see you again. Kiss the kids for me. Bye for now. More later.

All My Love,
Daddy

Image 15.1: Taking no chances. Charly couldn't reach us. Almost home.

HOME BUT NOT HEALED

The VC kept quiet and didn't bother our boats for my last few patrols. Thankfully! I left My Tho and arrived in Saigon without incident on July 2,1968. True to my word, I barely left my room on the 3rd floor of a hotel.

I dragged my sea bag onto the balcony and took out two new pairs of combat boots and three new jungle uniforms.

"I don't suppose I need these anymore. Good-bye, Vietnam. Good-bye!"

I threw them over the railing and onto the ground below. I returned to my room, closed the door, and symbolically left my memories of Vietnam behind me. For others who were leaving, they said goodbye in a much nastier way. They'd come out of their rooms and piss all over the place. It sounds gross I know, but compared to what we saw during our tours, it was no big deal.

My life patrolling the Mekong Delta in Vietnam was over. My life as a brown water sailor was over. My life living in and through a war was over. Thank God!

On the 5th of July, I was scheduled to leave Saigon on a Braniff commercial flight, but those plans got fouled up somehow.

Ten enlisted men and I boarded a military plane. I didn't care how we left Vietnam; I just wanted to get the hell out of the country. We rode in the cargo bay with the occupied caskets of 20 soldiers. You could say Vietnam spoke the final word, and the VC won the last battle.

That flight reminded me of the open wounds I suffered as I thought about SEAL Fraley, Lt. Dennis, Mhin, the other orphans, and so many military men, and civilians. Riding in the back of an uncomfortable cargo plane next to coffins was bittersweet. Twenty families would see a gray sedan pull into their driveway while I enjoyed the luxury of hugging my family. Although no physical wounds burdened me, I brought home internal scars that I couldn't explain, and no one would ever understand.

We eventually arrived at Travis Air Force Base, north of San Francisco. A *U.S. Navy* painted bus drove us to Treasure Island

Naval Base in San Francisco. As we drove through the Haight-Ashbury District, the hippie war protesters targeted the moving military bulls-eye with rocks or pounded the sides with their fists.

The last thing we needed after getting our butts blown off by VC snipers for a year was for our own people to hate us. Hearing rocks hit the bus shook me to the core because I thought I left all that crap behind in Vietnam.

The damn hippies cussed, spat, and called us "baby killers." I hated them for it. They didn't have the first clue of what we dealt with over there.

They lived comfortably on the mainland, exercising their right to protest, safe from danger. How the hell did they get freedom to gather and speak their minds? Soldiers and sailors fought and died to protect those rights and ensured every American was afforded those privileges. They were all a bunch of spoiled, stoned-out-of-their-mind, and ungrateful bastards. How dare they treat us like they did when none of it was our decision in the first place. Oh, they made me and everyone else on the bus mad.

Thankfully, I landed in Washington DC (not *Dulles* as originally planned) at night, and I wasn't with a big group that advertised my military duty in Vietnam. People in the airport recognized me as a serviceman, but no one gave me trouble. It was quite a different experience than out in California.

I never imagined I would see or complete such awful missions to survive in Vietnam. I simply reacted and responded to various circumstances and good people got exposed to bad situations. That's part of daily life during war.

As I decompressed, I felt sorry for the man I became. But, I tried to be a good husband and father to my family. Mike and Cathy were still quite young, and I didn't want to bring Vietnam home with me. I wanted them to know and love their pre-war daddy.

War reports filled the television air waves every night, but I saw enough live action for one lifetime, so I never watched.

For reasons beyond the scope of this book I won't explain why I never went on the *USS Albany* homeported at Boston. I spent the next 10 years of my service patrolling the blue water oceans around the world aboard a variety of ships based at Norfolk, Virginia.

Image 16.1: An oil painting of me and my three sweeties. It still hangs on our walls today.

Virginia became our home again, and I settled in with Joyce and my little family. The Navy gave me more opportunities to fulfill and achieve monumental goals as a quartermaster chief. Successfully navigating two different ships across the Atlantic Ocean, one to the Mediterranean Sea and the other to the Suez Canal are accomplishments I am incredibly proud of.

During my last 6-month cruise I told my CO, "After this hitch, I'm gone; I'll have my 20 in, and I'm out."

"What'ya gunna do? Leave me here. You're a good man, Smith. You gave a lot to this country and you deserve it."

I finished my Navy career on January 5, 1977 because I couldn't stand the open wounds of leaving my family anymore. Seeing their tears flow as they waved goodbye from a pier felt like blood gushing out of the gaping wound in my heart. The raw emotions and sadness I endured was tiring. No more separation and no more lengthy deployments.

I traded in patrolling the world's waterways for a new life. We left our Navy lives behind us in Virginia Beach and moved to Herndon, Virginia to begin a different and challenging career.

Although I voluntarily retired from working and living on the water, the Navy, and more specifically, the Vietnam War never left me. Short-timer's Syndrome plagues me to this day. The staccato barking of a dog down the street sounds eerily similar to a sniper's M-16 rifle shots. Sitting in the middle of a busy restaurant without a wall behind me and hearing a pile of plates crash in the kitchen makes me flinch in my chair.

What was that? Where did it come from? Are we being ambushed? Man your stations!

I sympathize and empathize with soldiers and sailors who order a few cocktails hoping to calm their frazzled nerves, so they can make it through a holiday dinner.

The casual observer and our own families can't possibly understand our discomfort, impatience, and inability to control our environment when we are out in public. They will never comprehend the hellish memories we live with daily.

War ruins marriages, relationships with children and families, and sadly, sometimes leaves military veterans with no suitable alternatives than to take their own lives.

On January 7, 1977, I donned a new uniform when I became a rookie officer for The U.S. Capitol Police Department. I spent eight weeks training at the FLETC Glynco Center between Savannah, GA and Jacksonville, FL, and another two months training at the Capitol. Lastly, I spent eight weeks training with the Capitol Police Field Officers.

I finished my last patrol and hung up my uniform for the final time on April 15, 1993, when I retired from the Capitol Police force.

I have been married to Joyce for over 57 years. Retirement treats us well and we enjoy a quiet life in the Panhandle of West Virginia, a few miles away from my son Mike and his wonderful wife Christine. They blessed us with three grandchildren. We visit Cathy, Peter, and our grand-doggies and grand-kitties every Thanksgiving in Connecticut.

Although my life has been good and continues to treat me well, I never closed the open wounds I sustained in 1967 and 1968.

I believe this book is the healing stitch I needed all along. Living with 50-year-old memories of war burdens my thoughts and emotions with an uncomfortable heaviness. The Navy gave me the proverbial cross to carry, but I didn't know how to relieve the weight on my shoulders, in my mind, and in my heart. Perhaps, in bringing this story to the surface, the darkness that quietly haunted me for a half century will disappear. I certainly hope so.

My initial goal was to put together a little chronology of my time in Vietnam to share only with my immediate family. However, Joyce, Cathy, and Peter helped me realize this story may have a far-reaching influence on all military families. I hope my fellow Vietnam soldiers and sailors will understand they are never alone in their struggle toward normalcy. I urge younger military families to seek the support you need to survive and thrive. Resources are now plentiful to help us all heal from PTSD and manage our other symptoms caused by war.

So please, take the necessary step to close your open wounds.

As it is late, and I am hungry, I will close and eat some chow; a hot bowl of stew sounds really nice right about now.

I'm damn sure ain't nobody gonna kick it over this time!

Bye for now.

QMC Robert W. Smith (Retired)

Open Wounds

INDEX

1. 1: Cagle, Paul Wayne. article.jpg, article1.jpg. PBR-FVA Gallery Home Page.
   http://pbr-fva.org/gallery2/main.php?g2_itemId=420,
   http://pbr-fva.org/gallery2/main.php?g2_itemId=423.
2. Intro.1: Wikimedia Commons. TUBS. 25 October 2011.
   https://commons.wikimedia.org/wiki/File:Mekong_Delta_in_Vietnam.svg.
   http://www.wikiwand.com/en/Operation_Game_Warden.
3. Image 1.1: U.S. Navy. riverine2.jpg. Small Arms Defense Journal.
   http://www.sadefensejournal.com/wp/?p=613.
4. Image 3.1: Warboats Of America. Wahler, Lee, image058. Warboats.org.
   http://www.warboats.org/StonerBWN/The%20Brown%20Water%20Navy%20in%20Vietnam_Part%202.htm.
5. Image 3.2: Naval History and Heritage Command. USN 1142259.tiff.
   https://www.history.navy.mil/content/history/nhhc/our-collections/photography/numerical-list-of-images/nhhc-series/nh-series/USN-1142000/USN-1142259.html
6. Image 4.1: Naval History and Heritage Command. 1399393725591.tiff.
   https://www.history.navy.mil/research/archives/digitized-collections/vietnam-war/united-states-naval-operations-vietnam-highlights-february-1966.html.
7. Image 4.2: Wikimedia Commons.220px-thumbnail.jpg. Penprapa Wut. 18 February 2011. Operation Game Warden - Wikiwand.com.
   http://www.wikiwand.com/en/Operation_Game_Warden.

8. Image 5.1: Smith, Robert W. image5.1.jpg. personal collection.

9. Image 5.2: Smith, Robert W. image5.2.jpg. personal collection.

10. Image 5.3: Smith, Robert W. image5.3.jpg. personal collection.

11. Image 5.4: Smith, Robert W. image5.4.jpg. personal collection.

12. Image 5.5: Smith, Robert W. image5.5.jpg. personal collection.

13. Image 6.1: Smith, Robert W. image6.1.jpg. personal collection.

14. Image 6.2: Smith, Robert W. image6.2.jpg. personal collection.

15. Image 6.3: NavSource Naval History. Harnett_County_AGP-821.jpg _www.navsource.org http://www.navsource.org/archives/10/16/1016082105.jpg.

16. Image 6.4: Stoner, Robert H. image056. Warboats.org. http://www.warboats.org/StonerBWN/The%20Brown%20Water%20Navy%20in%20Vietnam_Part%202.htm

17. Image 6.5: Naval History and Heritage Command. USN 1142263.tiff. https://www.history.navy.mil/content/history/nhhc/our-collections/photography/numerical-list-of-images/nhhc-series/nh-series/USN-1142000/USN-1142263.html

18. Image 7.1: Smith, Robert W. image7.1.jpg. personal collection.

19. Image 7.2: Naval History and Heritage Command. K-51442.tiff. https://www.history.navy.mil/content/history/nhhc/our-collections/photography/numerical-list-of-images/nhhc-series/nh-series/Other/K-51442.html

20. Image 7.3: UH-1E_of_HAL-3_escorting_PBRs_in_Vietnam_c1968.jpg. All Hands Magazine November 1968, p. 17. http://www.navy.mil/ah_online/archpdf/ah196811.pdf.

21. Image 7.4: Smith, Robert W. image7.4.jpg. personal collection.

22. Image 7.5: Smith, Robert W. image7.5.jpg. personal collection.

23. Image 7.6: Smith, Robert W. image7.6.jpg. personal collection.

24. Image 8.1: Naval History and Heritage Command. USN 1131566.tiff. https://www.history.navy.mil/content/history/nhhc/our-collections/photography/numerical-list-of-images/nara-series/usn/USN-1130000/USN-1131566.html.

25. Image 8.2: Morneault, Peter F. image8.1.jpg. personal collection.

26. Image 9.1: Smith, Robert W. image9.1.jpg. personal collection.

27. Image 9.2: Smith, Robert, W. image9.2.jpg. personal collection.

28. Image 10.1: Smith, Robert W. image10.1.jpg. personal collection.

29. Image 10.2: Smith, Robert W. image10.2.jpg. personal collection.

30. Image 10.3: Smith, Robert W. image10.3.jpg. personal collection.

31. Image 10.4: Smith, Robert W. image10.4.jpg. personal collection.

32. Image 11.1: U.S. Navy. UH-1E_of_HAL-3_with_PBR_in_Vietnam_c1967.jpg. All Hands Magazine. May 1967, p. 10. http://www.navy.mil/ah_online/archpdf/ah196705.pdf.

33. Image 11.2: Naval History and Heritage Command K-51441.tiff.
https://www.history.navy.mil/content/history/nhhc/our-collections/photography/numerical-list-of-images/nhhc-series/nh-series/Other/K-51441.html

34. Image 11.3: Smith, Robert W. image11.3.jpg. personal collection.

35. Image 11.4: Smith, Robert W. image11.4.jpg. personal collection.

36. Image 12.1: Smith, Robert W. image12.1.jpg. personal collection.

37. Image 12.2: Smith, Robert W. image12.2.jpg. personal collection.

38. Image 12.3: Naval History and Heritage Command. USN 1129450.tiff.
https://www.history.navy.mil/content/history/nhhc/our-collections/photography/numerical-list-of-images/nhhc-series/nh-series/USN-1129000/USN-1129450.html.

39. Image 13.1: Smith, Robert W. image13.1.jpg. personal collection.

40. Image 14.1: Smith, Robert W. image14.1.jpg. personal collection.

41. Image 15.1: Smith, Robert W. image 15.1.jpg. personal collection.

42. Image 16.1: Smith, Robert W. image 16.1.jpg. personal collection.

Made in the USA
Columbia, SC
22 December 2018